The MESA Way:

A Success Story of Nurturing Minorities for Math/Science-Based Careers

Wilbur H. Somerton, Mary Perry Smith,
Robert Finnell, and Ted W. Fuller

The MESA Way:
A Success Story of Nurturing Minorities
for Math/Science-Based Careers

By Wilbur H. Somerton, Mary Perry Smith,
Robert Finnell, and Ted W. Fuller

Copyright 1994 by the authors

Published by Caddo Gap Press
3145 Geary Boulevard, Suite 275
San Francisco, California 94118

List price: $17.95

ISBN 1-880192-10-1
Library of Congress Catalog Card Number 94-70617

Cover design by Susan Holtzer and Mason Jones
from photograph of Southern California MESA Day.
Text design and photographic arrangements
by Susan Holtzer and Ann Marie Hovie.

Library of Congress Cataloging-in-Publication Data

The MESA way : a success story of nurturing minorities for
  math/science based careers / Wilbur H. Somerton ... [et al.].
      p.   cm.
  Includes index.
  ISBN 1-880192-10-1 : $17.95
    1. Science--Vocational guidance. 2. Science--Vocational guidance-
  -California. 3. Mathematics--Vocational guidance. 4. Mathematics-
  -Vocational guidance--California. 5. Minority students--Vocational
  guidance. 6. Minority students--Vocational guidance--California.
  7. Mathematics, Engineering, Science Achievement Program--History.
  I. Somerton, Wilbur H.
  Q147.M47 1994
  510'.71'2794--dc20   94-4775
                                                            CIP

Table of Contents

Chapter 8—Industry Involvement with MESA 97

Funding by businesses provides the lifeblood, but loaned
executives and advisors show that industry's support goes
beyond self-interest.

Chapter 9—California Gets Involved 117

How MESA built legislative support and funding, and won
the endorsement of the California Post-secondary Education
Commission.

Chapter 10—Opting for Growth 129

Success at the high school level encourages outreach to
junior high, elementary and community college students,
plus a program of continuing support in universities.

Chapter 11—How Others View MESA 143

A Carnegie Corporation story puts the reader into a
classroom of MESA students.

Chapter 12—What the Future Holds 157

A growing emphasis at the community college level and a
program for American Indians are under way.

Chapter 13—Applying MESA Principles 163

These basic steps and sources of information will get you
started.

Reading to children at an early age and making them
aware of simple math concepts can go a long way
in preparing them for a MESA program.

Foreword

Excellence is Costly, But Mediocrity Costs Far More

By Glenn T. Seaborg

The now famous report "A Nation at Risk: The Imperative for Educational Reform," issued in 1983 by the National Commission on Excellence in Education, includes this recommendation:

> ...That schools, colleges, and universities adopt more rigorous and measurable standards, and higher expectations, for academic performance...

These educational mileposts—standards and expectations—have guided the significant steps taken by MESA (Mathematics, Engineering, Science Achievement) since its formation in 1970. As an active member of the Lawrence Hall of Science Advisory Council, I became involved with MESA in its first decade, an era of anxious soul searching by educators, parents, business people, and politicians. At that time, the need for such a program was obvious. African Americans, Hispanics, and Native Americans were conspicuously absent from college and university technical programs due to a lack of required pre-college math and science credits. The founders of MESA began a campaign, first in high schools and later in middle and elementary schools as well, convincing principals, teachers, parents, and students of the importance of raising standards. Nine out of ten MESA students went on to achieve those higher standards.

This book provides a blueprint. It profiles a few individuals—educators, business professionals and MESA staff—whose vision and hard work sculpted the program. The book (based on more than twenty years of experience) can serve as a how-to manual in conscripting educational allies and on the art of grantsmanship. It also includes problem-solving approaches that, if applied with imagination and zeal, might benefit the entire field of education.

MESA's discoveries may be of wider significance, however. Most MESA participants who went on to excel in college were only average students. Some were regarded as slow learners. As one MESA center director put it: "I do look at their scores and grade point averages... But I don't rely on scores. If I did I would miss a lot of talented kids." Often, it appears, the average students respond to the challenge, support, and discipline provided by the program. Leaders of industry might well ask if average employees would respond in like manner.

The MESA campaign continues today, capturing the interest of boys and girls motivated by career goals or their curiosity about math, science, or engineering. MESA encourages and helps underrepresented minorities through individualized attention, parental involvement, partnerships with businesses, support from like-minded youth, and money from private sources and the State of California. Borrowing a common practice of middle and upper class parents, MESA rewards good grade earners with cash incentives, which are usually spent on expenses, not treats. Teachers, college students, and industrial professionals donate time to tutor students. Field trips and summer employment offer a glimpse at the inner workings of industry.

Industry professionals have played a significant role in the development and

implementation of this program, offering suggestions, providing summer employment opportunities, leading field trips, loaning executives, tutoring students, serving on advisory boards, donating equipment and services, conducting teacher training sessions, speaking to students, and making financial contributions. Participating businesses recognize their support of MESA as an investment in a future work force better prepared to handle a technologically complex business environment. The success of MESA students has proven them right.

As a member of the National Commission on Excellence in Education (NCEE), I had an opportunity to explore the problems facing pre-college education in the United States. Our report, *A Nation at Risk*, warned:

> The educational foundations of our society are presently being eroded by a rising tide of mediocrity that threatens our future as a nation and as a people.

Glenn T. Seaborg
—Photo by John Jernegan

Some progress has been made in implementing the NCEE recommendations; unfortunately, national 1991 test scores, dropout rates, and teacher turnover rates make it clear that the remaining task is of monumental magnitude. For example:

Thirty percent of our high schools offer no courses in physics, 17 percent offer none in chemistry and 70 percent offer none in earth or space science.

Each year's class of dropouts costs the nation about $240 billion in crime, welfare, health care, and services. Put another way, we spend nine dollars to provide services for dropouts for each dollar spent on education.

Federal funding to train and retrain American workers has dropped more than 50 percent from its 1980 level of $13.2 billion.

Of all individuals entering the work force from now to the year 2000, only 15 percent will be white males. By then minorities and women will comprise about 82 percent of the work force.

Some people favor school choice as a solution to these problems, arguing that competition among schools will improve quality and reduce costs. School choice is not the answer, however, and may worsen the plight of minority students attending schools that are already underfunded.

Instead, government must identify the nation's educational needs, set standards, and then dramatically increase financial support of efforts to meet these goals. We must recognize education as an investment, not an expense.

Although school funding is traditionally a local or state responsibility, I am convinced change cannot be accomplished without federal help. This presents a sizeable problem. In a rational environment, such rising costs would be met by cuts in no-longer-needed military spending. Overall national security would be much enhanced if this federal money were devoted to civilian national security needs.

Here in California, we expect a more equitable taxation scheme than the well-intentioned but flawed Proposition 13 through which voters limited property taxes and sent a signal to legislators to stop evading their responsibilities. A healthy portion of those realigned property tax dollars belongs to the schools.

In the years to come, we predict greater participation and contributions by corporations and foundations. Finally, we hope for and expect state and federal government leaders to grasp the importance of education in this country's struggle to achieve the excellence of which it is capable.

We must work together, employing our considerable resources, to ensure a prosperous future. We should use successful designs like MESA's as models for teaching and motivating youth of varied backgrounds. Whatever the expense of improving science and mathematics education, this is an investment in the future we must make. Excellence is costly. But in the long run, mediocrity costs far more.

Preface

MESA intervenes in the lives of average, often uncommitted students who are underrepresented in university math-based fields. It nurtures them. It rewards them for success. The program began in 1970 and most of the students MESA has served have graduated from four-year colleges and universities. They're successful. More than half of them are women.

This account of the Mathematics, Engineering, Science Achievement program focuses on the often innovative efforts and praiseworthy results of the original high school program. A complete telling of MESA's story at the university level, the junior high activities, and the replications in fifteen other states, will require other books.

So, unless otherwise identified, the MESA program and events you are about to explore take place in California's high schools or in the Statewide Office or MESA centers around the state.

MESA sets high standards for its students and they must adhere to the program's key elements. One of the strengths of the program rests in the autonomy of its twenty centers serving high school students throughout the state. There is room for experimentation, innovation, and expansion of the program.

One MESA founder, when asked about its success in obtaining grants from foundations, the state, and corporations, replied, "The program is of such a quality and has produced such worthwhile results, it sells itself."

Another strength is the collaborative partnership between school districts, higher education institutions, the state, and industry.

"This is not a remedial program," goes the litany of high school teachers who serve as MESA advisors. They tell their students: "We expect the best of you, and we're going to help in every way possible so you can excel." That belief in the student's ability to achieve excellence undergirds the entire MESA effort.

As you read how it's done, we urge you to adopt or adapt the program if the students in your home or school aren't approaching their potential.

Over the years, hundreds of dedicated people, most of them volunteers, have been involved in the program. Equally dedicated paid staff go that extra mile to help their students. Throughout this book you will find many of these people mentioned, some because of their unusual contributions. One of the most difficult tasks faced by the authors was selecting those to be mentioned or profiled. We finally decided to name or profile those who had unique experiences in the various facets of the program. Many others could have been mentioned, and deservedly so, but limits had to be imposed. To those hundreds of other people, all of whom contributed so much to the success of the program, we offer our apologies and our heartfelt thanks.

The authors sincerely thank the Ernst D. van Loben Sels/Eleanor Slate van Loben Sels Charitable Foundation of San Francisco and its president, Claude H. Hogan, for not only providing the grants that got MESA started but also providing a grant to help finance research and preparation of the manuscript for this book. Thanks are also due Marion Diamond, director of the Lawrence Hall of Science, for the many services LHS provided. Fred Easter, executive director of MESA-California, and his staff have been most cooperative in providing data, facilities, and staff time for the preparation of the manuscript.

—WHS, MPS, RF, TWF

Dedications

Gene A. Houston
1940-1991

The pioneering efforts of Gene Houston established a MESA model at the university and college level, adapted from a program at California State University, Northridge. Working as a loaned executive from IBM, he began in 1982 drafting the plans, making the contacts, and instilling excitement about the benefits underrepresented minorities would realize from what was then known as the Minority Engineering Program and is now the MESA Minority Engineering Program. Sixteen of the programs were put in place under his leadership. He also served on MESA's Board of Directors.

A native of Austin, Texas, he attended Los Angeles City College, completed a tour of duty with the Air Force, and then began his IBM career. He filled key positions at its New York headquarters as one of the first African American executives there, serving as corporate manager of Personnel Resources and Director of Quality. As he advanced with the company, he

Gene A. Houston
—Photo by G. Clarke

moved forward with his education, receiving a Bachelor of Science degree from the University of San Francisco and a Master's degree from Pace University in New York. In San Francisco, he became regional manager for the company's U.S. Marketing and Services until his death on January 24, 1991.

Houston showed his community support through organizations such as Men of Tomorrow, Alpha Fraternity, and the Advisory Board of the Black Filmmakers Hall of Fame.

"Gene's warmth and caring touched us all," said Fred Easter, MESA's Statewide director. "His dedicated work to help underrepresented students will have a lasting impact for years to come."

Charles Tunstall
1949-1987

When Charles Tunstall didn't show up at his office Monday morning, September 14, 1987, staff members felt concerned, but decided he was meeting a student or solving a registration problem.

A week passed. University officials contacted the police, who said his locked car had been found three days after his disappearance, parked at San Francisco's Land's End area near the *USS San Francisco* memorial. The car was towed and police tried contacting Tunstall in vain.

His peers considered him the dean of Minority Engineering Program directors throughout California. Appointed director at UC Berkeley in 1983, he quickly established a leadership role in the network that later became the MESA Minority Engineering Program. His associates respected and admired him. Some called him "the miracle worker."

"He could talk to eighth graders, college deans, industry people, or fund-raisers," said Antoinette Torres, assistant director then. "Everyone loved him."

To his students, Tunstall was like a family. His life was wrapped in their welfare. He always found time for them.

"Charles gave doses of motivation," said Lawange Yonke, who graduated from UC's

Charles Tunstall

engineering program. "He kept an eye on us to make sure we were okay."

Tunstall devoted most of his time to students, but didn't abandon his love for art and jazz. When time permitted, he squeezed in a hike on a nature trail by himself. The solo hiking may have led to his death. It's likely he plunged from one of the difficult trails in the Seal Rocks/Land's End area near the spot where he parked his car. Police and a large group of his students and associates searched the area without turning up any evidence.

A meeting, held in a packed UC engineering auditorium, paid tribute to the man. Everyone had a "Charles story." From the comments, it was apparent he had touched the lives of all those present, but none so much as the students, the MESA MEP staff, faculty members and deans who worked with him. They openly shed the most tears that day.

Further Dedications

This book is further dedicated to MESA and MESA MEP staff, school advisors, and volunteers whose dedication and hard work are responsible for the the success of the MESA program.

MESA Centers:
California Polytechnic State University, San Luis Obispo
California State University, Bakersfield
California State University, Chico
California State University, Fresno
California State University, Long Beach
California State University, Los Angeles
California State University, Northridge
Capitol Center: California State University, Sacramento and University
    of California, Davis
Capitol Center: Mendocino County Satellite
Capitol Center: Sonoma County Satellite
Central Region/Cabrillo Community College
Harvey Mudd College
Loyola Marymount University
Mid-Peninsula Center: California State University, San Francisco
Mid-Peninsula Center: Foothill Community College, Los Altos Hills
Orange County Center: California State University, Fullerton and Uni-
    versity of California, Irvine

California State University, San Diego
California State University, San Francisco
California State University, San Jose
University of California, Berkeley
University of California, Santa Barbara
University of the Pacific
University of Southern California

MESA MEP Centers:
American River Community College, Sacramento
California Maritime Academy, Vallejo
California Polytechnic State University, San Luis Obispo
California State Polytechnic University, Pomona
California State University, Bakersfield
California State University, Chico
California State University, Fresno
California State University, Fullerton
California State University, Long Beach
California State University, Los Angeles
California State University, Northridge
California State University, Sacramento
California State University, San Diego
Califronia State University, San Francisco
California State University, San Jose
Cosumnes River College, Sacramento
Sacramento City College
Santa Clara University
University of California, Berkeley
University of California, Davis
University of California, Irvine
University of California, Los Angeles
University of California, San Diego
University of California, Santa Barbara
University of the Pacific
University of Southern California

Chapter 1
A Guidepost for Excellence

"I had no idea what an engineer was or what one did," says Sylvia Garcia. "We had no role models. Dad drove a truck and my mother worked as a clerk."

Then in 1981, her older brother, Raymond, joined a Gladstone High School group called Mathematics, Engineering, Science Achievement. As a youngster in Azusa, California, he had dreamed of becoming an astronaut and the MESA program offered special help with the math and science courses required for college admission.

At a MESA banquet for Raymond's group, Sylvia, attending in her ailing father's stead, wore her best dress. The boys who owned them, or could borrow them, wore suits and ties. Many of their parents attended and glowed as speakers praised their children.

"It turned me on," she recalls. "The next week, when the MESA center director invited me to take part in the program, I decided to follow in Raymond's footsteps."

Sylvia's parents, Rosemary and George Garcia, became involved when Raymond signed up. Since then, the couple has influenced nephews, nieces, and neighbors; about a dozen of them participated in MESA. Mrs. Garcia ran for the school board and served several terms.

Sylvia Garcia graduated from Harvey Mudd College and now writes software for Aerojet Electronics. Two sisters benefited from MESA: Rosemary is completing graduate work in communications and broadcasting at California State University, Fullerton, and Sandra is working on her master's in business administration while teaching. Raymond works as a fireman and plans to become a paramedic.

"We're typical of a lot of families that have children and cousins joining MESA," says Sylvia Garcia.

Aerojet underwrites the cost of her M.B.A. studies at Claremont Graduate School. She spends some of her spare time as a member of a consortium board that funds a Regional Occupational Program and youth groups.

"John Xavier, an '82 grad who works for Rockwell, and I are formalizing plans for a MESA alumni association," she says. "We think it'll be a great resource, especially in these difficult financial times when states, counties, and cities are cutting back.

"It's something I want to do," she adds. "I don't regard it as an obligation."

The Garcia family's experience underscores some of the benefits bestowed by the Mathematics, Engineering, Science Achievement secondary school program. The program helps underrepresented minority youngsters complete their preparatory requirements, gain admission, then earn their university or college degrees.

The MESA program started at Oakland (California) Technical High School in 1970 with twenty-five students. In 1993, the number of California secondary school students participating in MESA reached nearly 7,000 and the program influenced another 5,000 youngsters in elementary and junior high school. All told, more than 40,000 pre-college students took part from 1970 through 1992.

Seventy-three percent of MESA's California participants entered universities and colleges, compared with 13 percent of minorities at large. The retention rate of MESA students in the university segment of the program is 61 percent compared with less than 35 percent for other underrepresented minorities. These results probably exceed all other underrepresented minority engineering programs operating in the United States.

Some of MESA's pioneers see it as a small scale revolution that shows how the United States can achieve excellence in education. The main secrets of its success: high standards and nurture.

MESA began as a high school program. Now children as young as seven years of age talk about being astronauts or builders in school sessions with MESA staffers or volunteers. Gradually the students will learn what courses must be mastered to meet college requirements.

With others their age, MESA middle school students gather in study groups after school or at a summer session on a university campus. They discover it's okay to be bright and earn good grades.

In high school, teachers and counselors identify the boys and girls interested in math, engineering, or science and make sure they take more than algebra, geometry, and other courses college admission requires. They study trigonometry, chemistry, physics, and four years of English. On field trips, students explore the corporate work place with both the excitement and routine experienced by scientists and engineers.

Even in college, thanks to the MESA Minority Engineering Program, they find support and a sense of community with other students.

A big amount of nurturing comes from industry. It was its need for minorities trained in technical fields that spawned MESA in 1970. Twenty years later, corporations and foundations had contributed nearly $14 million, or 42 percent, of the total funds for the program.

John A. Young explains this generosity. The retired president and chief executive officer of Hewlett Packard Company says: "The two most significant competitive advantages any company can develop are technology and people. MESA plays an invaluable role in bringing these two together and in tapping the pool of students who will become our future scientists and engineers."

MESA's Statewide Office helps make it happen with funds from major companies and foundations. It also coordinates the training of center directors and special events for students and teachers from all sections of the state.

The Basic Program

How do teachers select students who can blossom in the high school Mathematics, Engineering, Science Achievement program?

The African American, Mexican American, Native American, or Puerto Rican youth already are enrolled in or willing to take algebra in ninth grade and, in the next two years, geometry, trigonometry, pre-calculus, chemistry, physics, and English. They also voice an interest in careers in science or engineering.

Family income doesn't affect participation. Most MESA students are earning average grades when they start. That's when the nurturing slips into high gear. Here's how:

1. **Group study sessions**—Students help one another.

2. **Academic advising**—Busy high school counselors are fortunate if they find time to advise students who show an interest in college. Students interested in mathematics-related careers and especially those from low-income families, were graduating without discovering much about college pre-requisites for these majors. So MESA advisors filled the breach. They uncovered the youngsters' career goals, described the courses needed along the way, and introduced them to the colleges and universities that meshed with their goals. The MESA advisors are math and science teachers who use MESA staff and advisory board members, high school counselors, and professional engineers as resources.

3. **Study assistance**—Volunteers from industry, plus MESA alumni, college students and advanced MESA students, tutor the youth. Many students represent the first members of their families graduating from high school. Often they bump

into roadblocks, so the development of study skills is an important element of MESA students' study sessions. Typically, study sessions at a high school take place after school Monday through Thursday. Teachers also help, providing encouragement or a sympathetic ear.

4. Extra study bonuses—In the summer of 1992, a six-week session attracted 120 middle school students and the "Precollege Academy" drew 160 high schoolers to the UC Berkeley campus. Here and at most of the nineteen other MESA centers, teachers make math and science fun as well as interesting during the summer. Youngsters form friendships and equip themselves with better study habits.

Once a year, MESA Day brings students together for a regional blend of contests, such as building the strongest bridge or oil derrick out of toothpicks, picnicking, and fun.

MESA student constructing toothpick derrick

MESA students also gather after school for joint study sessions and, on Saturdays, for academies, and for building friendships and study skills.

5. Incentive awards—Giving students money for good grades caused a flap when MESA first sought state funding help. "You're rewarding students for doing what they're supposed to do," was a common reaction. Senior high students who win cash awards, usually ranging from $100 to $250 a year, earn at least two A's and a B in advanced math, science, and English courses. "This is exactly what middle and upper income parents do for their students. . ." MESA's first executive director, Robert Finnell, told the California legislature when seeking state funding. He added that cash incentives showed the whole school that hard work brought rewards. By the 1980s, cash was an accepted incentive in many of the nation's high schools.

6. Pulling in the parents—The MESA advisor usually opens the gate, then, with the help of the rest of the MESA team, helps draw parents into the program, motivating them to become their children's cheerleaders and advocates. Their interest and support give students an added boost for the arduous long haul. MESA's influence often alters the views of school administrators who sometimes

MESA students from Berkeley, on field trip to PG&E nuclear facility at Diablo Canyon, are briefed by PG&E vice president James Schiffler

regard parents only as sources of interruption and evidence of disciplinary problems.

7. Field trips—On a catwalk above a refinery reforming facility or in the test lab of a research center, students glimpse the types of opportunities and challenges available in scientific and technical fields. Employees and executives who guide the visitors answer questions using the latest figures and newest procedures. Youngsters pay attention when a chief executive officer takes time to chat in a well-appointed board room.

8. Summer jobs—Normally this involves a small percent of MESA's students. Employers usually require that temporary help be at least sixteen years old, which rules out most high school freshmen and sophomores. Those juniors and seniors who do work broaden their know-how on science-related matters and the nitty gritty of resumes and employment interviews. They discover types of work they enjoy or dislike. They also earn some money, which often helps pay family expenses. The summer jobs also give employers a preview of prospective permanent employees of the future.

Any young person who receives this sort of nurturing should excel at school, you may be thinking.

Exactly.

The next question: If that's what it takes for excellence in education, what's the cost?

MESA-California in 1992-93 spent about $200 per secondary school student for the year. This includes administrative expenses and salaries of eighty-one staff members statewide, including center directors at each participating university. To put this in perspective, the cost of repairing the damage caused by the Los Angeles riots alone would fund one million MESA students for four years.

Advantages of Growth

MESA executive director Fred Easter says, "The organization has grown in terms of students served while shrinking in terms of personnel and overall budget."

His plans call for including the state's community college system in MESA's network in a major way. This means expansion of the college level MESA Minority Engineering Program and its nurturing and structure.

"MESA must be extended to many more school sites," Easter says, in response to the mandate implicit in the California legislation that requires a MESA-type program in schools with 40 percent or more of their enrollment made up of underrepresented minorities. (As of 1993, the legislature had not funded the measure.)

The ultimate goal for MESA is self-destruction. That's the view of Wilbur Somerton, UC Berkeley engineering professor and cofounder of the program. The founders hope the day will dawn when society values education and parents instill their children with self-esteem; when teacher-to-student ratios decrease and teachers have time for in-service updates on rapidly changing technology; when students obtain help as they hit roadblocks and rise to perform at their potential.

Until that day, many of the nation's schools can benefit by using MESA's approach to establish high standards and its methods of nurturing students, according to its founders. The program's progress chart shows peaks and valleys typical of any organization, but it was a peak, surprisingly, that almost proved its undoing. More about that in Chapter 5.

Gary Long:
Finding the Right Path

"I grew up in an area of Los Angeles where there were no engineers, no professionals," says Gary Long. "I didn't know what engineers did, but, growing up, I wanted to be an astronaut, to build things, so I knew that was the field for me."

At John Muir Junior High, math and science piqued his interest, then a MESA advisor came in for a visit.

"I thought I needed B's and C's to get into college," Long says. "But it turned out I needed A's—plus trigonometry, precalculus, and physics. I wasn't sure what path to take."

At Manual Arts High School, math teacher Jessie Davis guided the lad. William Wu, University of Southern California MESA Center director, helped him set priorities.

"Willie Wu's recommendation made it possible for me to conduct research at a UCLA lab with thirty top high school students from around the country, thanks to a National Science Foundation program."

Late in 1991, Long became an assistant professor of mechanical and aerospace engineering at the University of California, Irvine.

Gary Long

He's the first MESA graduate to achieve professorial rank. UC's strong emphasis on research gives him time to explore interests in robotics, automation and bio-mechanics.

"Two of my graduate students are designing a robot and another is developing a master controller—a super joy stick that will help the operator feel what's happening to the robot."

An ardent runner, cyclist, and weight lifter, Long, as faculty advisor, devotes time to the university's branch of the National Society of Black Engineers and serves on a UC Irvine MESA steering committee formed in 1991, just a few months after he was named an assistant professor. When there's time for reading, he chooses something in the metaphysical realm or sci-fi books by authors like Timothy Zahn.

"Growing up, life is a fantasy," he says. "For some people it remains that way, but you begin to feel like contributing to society. I'm picking areas directly applicable to society."

As for MESA's help along the way, he says, "I definitely knew I was going to be an engineer, although as a kid I didn't even know what an engineer did. Being in the MESA program made it a lot easier. It helped me set priorities."

Marlene Watson:
A Whole New World Opens

At the age of thirteen, Marlene Watson opened a karate class and taught thirty students ranging in age from seven to adult. She earned her black belt when she reached fifteen. She liked drawing and this led to a part-time job for the Alameda (California) Naval Air Station's drafting department.

With initiative like this, she gravitated toward MESA and became one of the first American Indians in the program.

"Mary Perry Smith was my geometry teacher in 1977 at Oakland Tech High," she says. "I didn't have any idea of what I wanted to be, so I finally decided engineering technician would be my goal. She encouraged me to take as much math and physics as I could."

Watson graduated at the age of sixteen, enrolled at the University of California, Berkeley, with a major in civil engineering, and switched to architecture in her junior year. After graduating in 1985, she worked three years, then returned to UC for a master's degree in architecture and, in December 1992, another in civil engineering.

One source of educational help was UC's Saturday Professional Development Program. "PDP taught us the terminology of the work place and basic principles, like the importance of being on time."

In a busy senior high school year, Watson received the shock treatment—an F in trigonometry in the first grading period.

"Mary Perry Smith was concerned," says Watson. "I stayed up until 2 a.m. every night and ended up with a B+ in the course."

Marlene Watson (right) during MESA Day at CSU Sacramento

—Photo by John Jernegan

Field trips to places like Hewlett-Packard helped spark an interest in computers, machines that today enable her to "build" a three dimensional model of a building.

Her recollections of MESA include the camaraderie.

"We worked in groups, which helped you identify with other students. It gave you a little extra effort."

Watson's parents divorced when she was five years old; her mother died in 1988. "She encouraged my two brothers, my sister, and me to go to school, and gave us time to study," Marlene Watson recalls. "Both of my brothers are carpenters and their work got me interested in older homes, the value of wood in design, and the aesthetics of buildings."

After high school, a summer threshold program provided a review of algebra, trigonometry, geometry, and English, "And this definitely helped."

The field of architecture ". . .opened a whole new world for me," Watson says. She enjoys initiating new designs, developing energy efficient plans, and her diverse background enables her to understand the construction management aspects of a project. As a member of Vision Enterprises, she works with American Indian reservation leaders, designing community centers and other projects in California. She is active at the national level in organizations working for American Indian causes.

"I am fighting for the rights of my people for housing, medical care, and social activities," Watson says.

The Hernandez Family: Giving Something Back

"School came first, jobs and chores around the house second," says Greg Hernandez. "Once you were finished with homework, then you could do everything else."

Growing up in Azusa, California, with eight brothers and sisters, he absorbed the message that education offered change and empowerment. Jessie and Johnny Hernandez scraped along on his pay as a pipe fitter so that seven of their children could obtain university degrees. And MESA played a key role in those accomplishments.

The parents inspected each report card. A grade of B was cause for serious discussion, because good grades paved the avenue to scholarships, which were passports to professional careers.

Greg Hernandez echoes those thoughts in his job as a math teacher at Gladstone High School, the clan's alma mater. He also coaches cross country and track.

The Hernandez Family (top row—Lupe, John, Johnny Sr., Martha, Jessie, Frank, Claudia, and Gregory; bottom row— Edward, Alejandro, and Robert) photographed at Martha's wedding

"MESA's incentive awards pushed me to get good grades," says Greg, who served as class valedictorian. "I didn't have to find a job. There was time for school and for cross country."

He majored in computer science at UCLA, switched to math, and graduated in 1989 with help from the MESA Minority Engineering Program (MESA MEP), a college level support program.

"I worked for MESA MEP during the school year and they let me rearrange my work schedule whenever I needed extra time for study," he says. A summer computer programming job convinced him he'd rather be working with people, and an enjoyable stint at tutoring suggested that teaching might be his calling, which led him back to Gladstone High, a school made up mostly of Hispanics.

"I'm teaching MESA kids again this summer at Harvey Mudd College, so the program helped me as a student and now it pays me for doing something I thoroughly enjoy," he says.

He and his brothers and sisters established a Gladstone High scholarship in memory of their father, who died in 1984. It's helping Hispanic students head for the college of their choice.

UCLA won out as the choice of the Hernandez offspring even though dad rooted for USC. Only Martha, the oldest, deviated by graduating from UC Santa Barbara, majoring in dramatic arts and bilingual education. She's the principal now for two Santa Paula School District schools. Her success inspired the rest of the children while at the same time providing her parents with knowhow on scholarships, applications and requirements of universities.

John Hernandez graduated from UCLA in 1978 and teaches science for a Los Angeles School District school in Huntington Beach. He's been honored by Los Angeles mayor Tom Bradley and the National Association for the Advancement of Colored People for educational leadership among youth of various ethnic groups.

Lupe Hernandez, now the mother of four, coordinates catechism for her Azusa Catholic church.

Frank Hernandez, a computer programmer, graduated from UCLA in 1983.

Ed Hernandez obtained his B.S. degree in kinesiology in 1984 and became a physician after graduating from UCLA's School of Medicine in 1988.

Claudia Hernandez, another UCLA graduate, was working on her Ph.D. in a Michigan pharmacy school in 1992.

Robert Hernandez graduated from UCLA in 1991, then enrolled in its medical school. "My family was the example for me," he says. "I knew when and how and where to take tests and how to get around in the university bureaucracy because my older brothers and sisters gave me advice."

Alejandro Hernandez enrolled at UCLA in 1992 after acquiring his high school math training from his brother Greg.

The Hernandez family's sons and daughters have something in common: the scholarship honoring their father. Daughter Martha puts it this way: "We felt that we not only needed to honor the memory of our father, but we needed to give something back by helping those students who need that little push."

Several of them also participate in MESA activities. "We all benefited from MESA," says Greg Hernandez.

His father died in 1984, a victim of prolonged asbestos exposure on the job.

"My husband probably would have wanted to go on with school," recalls his widow. "But his grandmother was anxious for him to get out so he could go with the family and pick oranges." He became an ardent USC sports fan and vowed to give his children the opportunity to earn degrees and become successful—all because of USC. When seven of them ended up at UCLA instead, he gave his full support and encouragement except when the two schools met on the football field or diamond.

And after encouraging, helping, and nurturing nine children to excel in school, Jessie Hernandez still gives a nudge to those around her; she works as an adult education assistant.

Students at 1993 central California MESA Day at CSU Fresno

Chapter 2
Filling the Need

"We need qualified people with training in scientific and technical fields."
Industry and government employers voiced this necessity in the 1960s. They
saw Japan and Germany training far more engineers and scientists than the
United States. They also noted the lack of minorities in these fields, mainly
because the minority student had not been steered toward the calculus-based
fields in college.

After civil rights legislation passed in the mid-Sixties, "affirmative action"
became a popular buzz term. New programs evolved with funding from a variety
of sources, including the federal government. Some of them succeeded in easing
problems endured by minority groups over long stretches of history. Many
programs failed, however. They addressed the wrong problem or based their
approaches on misunderstood causes of the problems.

Civil rights legislation, enacted in 1965, helped motivate industry recruiters.
They vied for technically trained minority university graduates, who became
conspicuous by their absence. Industry executives began asking university
professors about the dearth of qualified minorities, particularly African-American, Mexican-American, Native-American, and Puerto Rican graduates. Federal
Manpower Commission data showed relatively few minority professionals worked
in technical/scientific fields. These same data revealed a shortfall in the number
of trained personnel to meet the needs of industry and government. There was talk
of encouraging immigration of skilled technical personnel from abroad. Even in
the Sixties this seemed ludicrous in light of a large, nearly untapped U.S.
resource: its growing minority population.

In 1993, California's changing demographics indicated the minority population will become a majority early in the next century. But, for the state's continued growth in high technology, employers may still need trained workers from overseas, especially if the education system remains unchanged.

"Why not take advantage of California's untapped resources?" ask the people involved in Mathematics, Engineering, Science Achievement. "Support the improved education and training of minority group students. Then these students who invest the time and effort may proudly enter the mainstream of modern technology. That's what MESA is all about."

EOP Debuts

In 1966 a faculty committee at the University of California, Berkeley, studied the lack of minority group students entering the university. The committee members recommended to Chancellor Roger Heyns a program that would significantly increase the number of minority students. He agreed to the proposal and hired Bill Somerville as a special assistant to establish what later became known as the Educational Opportunity Program (EOP). Somerville first visited 120 California high schools, assessing the problem and recruiting minorities for a College Commitment Program. In this program, university students visited high schools as assistant counselors, helping prepare minority students for the university admission hurdles.

Between 1966 and 1968 the EOP team recruited more than 1,000 students who enrolled at UC Berkeley. Some did not meet the admission requirements, but, if they showed potential, they gained admission under a "2 percent rule" used extensively for admitting promising athletes. On-campus tutors assisted these students in their studies.

Ninety-nine out of a hundred of the African-American students enrolled in social science courses for majors in social welfare-type programs. The reason? Many of them said, "I want to help my people." Another reason centered on their lack of high school courses in advanced mathematics and science. In many cases, the students' high school counselors had steered them away from "difficult" courses, suggesting that the inevitable C's and D's, which some would get, would jeopardize their university admission opportunities. In addition, the lack of money and the lack of family tradition often excluded or even downplayed higher education.

EOP received frequent and favorable publicity. Faculty members at Berkeley heard about it and some came forward, offering assistance. One of these, engineering professor Wilbur "Bill" Somerton, simply asked, "Why aren't we getting EOP students in engineering?"

"They're not prepared to take calculus," Somerville replied, "and nothing's changed since you were in school: without calculus you don't become an engineer." Somerton was intrigued and joined others in a search for a solution.

Paltry Percentages for "Hard" Science

When the MESA program began, the enrollment of minority group students in colleges and universities had increased in the previous ten years from about 3 percent to nearly 5 percent. At the University of California, Berkeley, the number increased from 2 percent to 3 percent of the total student body over the same period of time, and the underrepresented minority enrollment in scientific and technical fields was a dismal 1.5 percent of the number enrolled in these fields. Nationwide, the representation of these minorities in the "hard" sciences was less than 2 percent.

In 1967, Beth Cobb, a concerned resident of Berkeley, volunteered her services to EOP. As administrator of the Moribito 49er Scholarship Program, funded by the San Francisco Foundation, she had made a special effort to reach minority youth. In her EOP role she proposed a University of California "Incentive Scholarship Program." It contained the key elements of the Mathematics, Engineering, Science Achievement program that was to follow.

"Let's provide immediate, tangible financial rewards so these students won't have to work at part-time jobs," she said. "Ask the teachers to select students with college potential that isn't being realized."

During an early recruiting visit to Woodrow Wilson Junior High School in Oakland, Bill Somerton gave a talk about MESA to a group of eighth grade students, most of whom were African-American. Afterwards, one student asked him, "Do you mean to tell me I don't have to push a broom the rest of my life?"

"No, of course not," Somerton said. "What would you like to do if you had a choice?"

"I'd like to be an electrician," the lad said.

"Why not an electrical engineer?"

The student shook his head, unable to conceive this happening.

As Somerton visited other schools, he stirred sparks of interest, encouraging students.

"Tell me what you'd like to do after finishing school?" he asked. After they expressed their hopes for the future, he explained how they could realize their hopes and dreams through MESA and their own hard work.

"We could focus efforts on making academic achievement prestigious, especially when it leads to college admission," Beth Cobb said. She also suggested field trips for students, visits by the program coordinator with their families, and regular discussion sessions where students could learn together.

Somerville and Somerton, with help from physics professors Alan Portis and Harry Morrison, tailored Beth Cobb's model for the math and science areas. Early

The 1982 MESA team—Gene Houston, Mary Perry Smith,
Wilbur "Bill" Somerton, Vinetta Jones-Sykes, and Robert Finnell (left to right)

students in the program dreamed up the name Mathematics, Engineering, Science Achievement Awards Program, which they quickly converted to MESSUP. Cobb wrote a funding proposal and Somerville and Somerton visited company executives who still complained about the lack of qualified minority job candidates. When asked for financial support, the industrialists hesitated. "We'll wait until you establish a track record," was the standard response. Somerville then submitted the proposal to the Van Loben Sels Foundation in San Francisco. It bestowed a grant of $15,000 and MESA was on its way.

The Educational Opportunity Program staff had established good contacts with high school teachers. One teacher, David Stonerod at Oakland Technical High School, lent a hand and did MESA a favor by recommending a colleague, Mary Perry Smith. (See page 28 for her profile.) Her concern about the paucity of minority students in her advanced math classes led her naturally to embrace the MESA concept. With an assist from Beth Cobb, she worked out the high school's side of the program while selecting the first twenty-five students who showed interest and potential for math-based higher education.

"MESA enhances the self-worth of the students," Smith said. "They set high career goals for themselves and they get support along the way. That support includes individual counseling by trained staff people, tutoring and peer study groups."

From its start in 1970 through 1992, MESA in California served more than 40,000 minority group students in 250 elementary, middle, and high schools. Fifteen other states now use the MESA model or an adaptation of it. In 1991, the California program began expanding to community colleges. In spite of this impressive growth, MESA reaches only 4 percent of the eligible students in California.

"Seventy-three percent of MESA's students enroll in four-year colleges or universities," says Fred O. Easter, Jr., MESA Statewide executive director. "In comparison, only 13 percent of the total underrepresented minority students in California enroll. The MESA students' graduation rate equals or, in some cases, exceeds that of the current majority group students in four-year educational institutions.

"Hundreds of volunteers helped make these impressive statistics possible. A dedicated professional staff maintains the program's high quality, sometimes in spite of people who would lower standards in the name of 'compassion,'" Easter says.

Funding, oftentimes a problem with such programs, has not been unusually difficult for MESA, according to Bill Somerton (see Chapters 6 and 7). "MESA established a good track record and it carefully documents statistics on the progress of students. This brought in funds at levels that allowed phased expansion of the program.

"One major funding source threatened to discontinue its support unless we expanded MESA statewide," Somerton says. "The message came loud and clear. Although we feared the possible negative effects of rapid expansion on the quality of the program, needless to say, we expanded statewide."

The big contributors include the state, industry, foundations and a few school districts.

What about the future?

"We need to triple the size of the program by 1995 to help meet the anticipated needs for trained, qualified technical personnel," Bill Somerton says. "To meet the needs of minorities in other professional fields, the program would need to be increased by a factor of ten."

Bill Somerton (right) presenting —Photo by P. Clarke
plaque to Lodwrick Cook

Bill Somerton: Sticking Around for the Long Haul

In the late 1960s, recruiters from three different oil companies asked Bill Somerton, "Where are your qualified, technically trained minority graduates?" The petroleum engineering professor at UC Berkeley responded, "I don't know, but I'll try to find out." Each fall requests poured in for petroleum engineering graduates.

This was shortly after passage of federal civil rights legislation and companies anxiously sought their share of qualified minority graduates. Somerton discovered less than 1 percent of the engineering graduates came from underrepresented minority groups. Wondering why, he contacted Bill Somerville, then director of the university's Educational Opportunity Program. Under EOP, the university had successfully recruited minority group students for university admission. Although most of them met minimum admission requirements, by and large they lacked high school preparation to enter math-based fields of study. Somerton joined with Somerville and other university and high school techers and staff members to create the program now known as MESA.

Wilbur H. Somerton has stuck with MESA in one role or another for more than twenty years while most of the other founders made their contribution then pursued other interests.

What made him stick?

"I knew we had a good program going which would help solve an important problem," he says. "It just needed watching and nurturing to assure its continuing success."

Somerton has served in many roles, most importantly, as the program's first faculty advisor. He served as advisory board chairman, later headed the Expansion Committee, then became the first chairman of the MESA board of directors. He also served as the university's principal investigator for the MESA program and had overall responsibility for minority programs in UC's College of Engineering, which he served as assistant dean.

"Although I enjoyed all of my associations with MESA, I enjoyed it most when I worked more directly with the operation of the program: arranging student field trips to various industries and engineering firms; helping students get summer jobs; developing and helping conduct their contests, such as the toothpick oil derrick contest; arranging for my own students to help in tutorials; and securing funding of the program.

"I was born in Canada, but my family moved to California when I was in the first grade. I graduated from Long Beach Poly High and what I remember most about that was the 1933 earthquake. I'd had classes all afternoon under the dome of the administration building. A couple of hours later, that dome ended up in the basement."

Somerton received all of his university training at UC Berkeley. He started in civil engineering, changed to geology and finally found his niche in petroleum engineering. He received his B.S. degree, then, while waiting for a commission in the Navy during World War II, earned his M.S. degree. During this time he was on leave from an oil company and fully intended going back after the war.

"Shortly before my separation from active duty, I received a cable from the university asking me to come back and help teach during the GI bulge," Somerton says. He continued with advanced graduate work and earned the degree of petroleum engineer. Somerton retired as head of the petroleum engineering program in 1987 after more than forty years of service.

Since then, the slender, five-foot, nine-inch resident of Lafayette, California, participated in the first American/Soviet peace walk in Russia just days after his retirement. He spent ten weeks in China on a lecture tour under the sponsorship of the Chinese Ministry of Petroleum. He spent several weeks working with universities in Hanoi. In the fall of 1992, he and his wife, Irma, returned to Vietnam where he lectured at the universities while she worked with women's and children's groups.

In addition to traveling, Somerton recently completed a technical book and made a major contribution to this one.

"Irma and I are amateur genealogists and we've traced the Somerton family back to the Mayflower," he says.

She is a professional research librarian and has guided the study that has taken them to many parts of the U.S., Canada and Europe. Their six children and nine grandchildren keep life for them anything but dull.

—Photo by John Jernegan

Teacher with students at MESA Day activity

Chapter 3
Out of Turmoil
Comes Transition

At the beginning of the Sixties, more than 60 percent of Oakland Technical High School's graduating seniors were white. Half of them came from middle and upper-middle income families. Its racial mix of African-American, Caucasian, and Asian students almost matched the city's makeup.

Prior to 1968, most of Tech's students skillfully juggled political activism with their studies and some traditional high school activities. Some took part in excellent extracurricular activities sponsored by strong departments in music, drama, foreign language, business, and math. The school supported two choral groups, an orchestra, and a band, as well as eleven clubs.

The Drama Department mounted spring and fall productions. Students could also compete in swimming, tennis, soccer, gymnastics, and wrestling, along with the traditional track, baseball, football, and basketball teams.

By 1969, Tech's graduating class was less than 15 percent white. As the number of African-American and Asian students increased, more white families sent their children to private or out-of-district schools. During that same period, Asian graduates increased from less than 5 percent to nearly 15 percent. Additionally, about 5 percent of Tech's students came from other countries and learned their English in the "International Classes."

Specific events altered the racial mix of the school's student body. Tech stayed rather tranquil through the assassinations of John F. Kennedy, Malcolm X, and Robert Kennedy, even though these events affected the attitudes and eventually the lives of many students. The assassination of Martin Luther King, Jr., on Thursday, April 4, 1968, however, elicited a different reaction.

The Oakland schools' superintendent did not issue districtwide instructions to the principals, so the next morning it was every school for itself. The Berkeley Schools' superintendent, on the other hand, had worked with his principals far into the night, planning how to open and operate their schools on April 5.

At Tech, when "school as usual" began, students convened an impromptu memorial service in the football stands. Afterwards they shut down the school by systematically opening classroom doors and yelling, "School is out." Some attacked Caucasian students and smashed windows and furniture.

"It was Tech's first student riot; a frightening experience to observe and be trapped in," says Mary Perry Smith, a math teacher and MESA's first advisor. "When school opened in September, 1969, 'white flight' transformed the Tech student body. It became a nearly 90 percent non-white population."

In the Eye of the Storm

Assassinations were not the only events that helped make Tech students children of the Sixties. They lived with and were surrounded by political and social movements influencing the entire country. The Free Speech Movement at the University of California, Berkeley, and anti-Vietnam War demonstrations at the Army Induction Center in downtown Oakland took place within blocks of their homes. Black Panthers, riot police, and state troopers marched and drove up and down streets where Tech students played baseball. The Black Panthers organized its headquarters nearby. Tech graduates, including Huey Newton from the Class of 1961, were among the founders, leaders, and members of this group.

"The rebellion against the establishment was not lost on our students," Smith says.

The January 23, 1969, issue of Tech's student newspaper, *Scribe News*, carried a front-page story on the student strike at San Francisco State. A headline story described the Board of Education meeting at which student body leaders from Oakland's six high schools laid out these demands:

1. Re-educate teachers, counselors, and administrators and sensitize them to the needs of African-American, Mexican-American, Native-American, and Asian students.
2. Integrate minority history into required social studies, rather than optional, elective courses.
3. Make sure textbooks related to the needs of minorities.

"It's interesting to note in the Nineties the issues about which our students were passionate during the late Sixties are still around," says Smith, who joined the Tech faculty in 1961. "These demands shifted to the ivory towers of colleges and universities where, as hotly debated topics among faculty, students, and administrators, they continue to cause turmoil."

The New Breed

These political and social movements, along with the political violence of the Sixties, produced politically aware and active students. For five years, from 1966 through 1969, Tech began each school year with a different principal. Traditionalists, unaccustomed to being accountable to students, collided with Tech students involved with their own education who spoke out on the school's problems. The students staged protests, demonstrating their interest in participating in faculty and staff planning sessions dealing with Tech's educational and social problems.

"In general, they refused to be treated like traditionally voiceless students," Smith says. "Principals who could not deal with these vocal students exited through Tech's revolving door."

Tech Selected for First MESA Program

MESA, headquartered in UC Berkeley's Lawrence Hall of Science, picked Tech for its first program for several reasons. The high school, just a short distance away, served as the traditional site for the University's School of Education high school summer program. UC's summer school teachers came from districts around the San Francisco Bay Area and the School of Education trained its student teachers and experimented with new teaching techniques and materials in these programs. This close connection generated ideas Tech faculty members passed along for comment or use in experimental programs. Most of the programs lasted less than a year, often because funds ran out or, worse, after promises to students and teachers and hours of planning and hoping, programs died aborning because funds never materialized.

"During the spring of 1969, Bill Somerville interviewed me and other math teachers and our black students enrolled in college-prep math," recalls Smith. "As the director of UC's Educational Opportunity Program, he asked, 'Why don't more of these students major in math, engineering, and science in college?'

"He listened to our answers. He also asked our opinions of a program for which he was trying to get funding."

In 1970, Tech's faculty still felt positively toward education, something often lacking in inner-city schools, according to Smith.

"Tech's academically talented, relatively young teachers had not burned out on the problems of educating all of the people's children," she says. "The school had a good mix of academically able students even though most of them came from low-income homes. A majority of them planned on attending two- or four-year colleges. They were using education to improve their lives."

A competitive number of Tech students graduated from UC Berkeley. Each

Math Department teacher agreed to supervise after-school study sessions at least two days a month. Students in advanced college-prep math classes earned extra points on their homework each time they stayed after school to tutor students in other classes. Student teachers helped supervise these study sessions. These activities were in place at Tech when Wilbur "Bill" Somerton, a UC engineering professor, and Somerville started searching for a MESA start-up school.

The MESA program started at Tech at an opportune time. It gave needed direction to students with academic ability but little knowledge about exploiting it for their own and society's benefit.

William Miller, Tech's principal in 1969, invited Smith to his office.

"I want you to work with Mr. Somerville and others at UC to implement a new program," he said. "It's designed to attack the problem of underrepresentation of minority professionals in math and the sciences. I'd like you to be the school's advisor."

"As the advisor," Smith recalls, "my role was to start a pilot program, see if it helped our students, and to suggest any changes that would bring about positive results. Since cash incentives seemed a critical element, I insisted these awards be funded for at least three years, enough time for the original group of students to graduate."

Student Selection

What process to use for selecting students?

At Tech, the initial screening process proved easy. For several years, the Math Department had asked its students to complete a questionnaire. It revealed information about their current classes, hobbies, educational goals, and career plans. Teachers used the results for career-based awards and scholarships, plus advising students on their math class selections.

"We chose advanced math, geometry, and algebra II students interested in math and science for further review," says Smith. "For the final selection, I checked test scores in the counselors' files, a practice we later dropped. It proved less effective than combining student interest with their math grades.

"We enthusiastically described MESA to our first group. They were in grades 10, 11, and 12 during the spring semester of 1970. These were students enrolled in academic math classes beyond first-year algebra, interested in math and science careers or activities, and were passing their current subjects."

The student selection philosophy has proved accurate over the years. Here's why:

MESA insists on high academic standards that encourage and support outstanding performance. It is not a remedial program. The founders saw the federal government putting billions of dollars into remedial efforts while ignoring the average student who plugged along, passing grade-level math, science, and English classes.

Students who cannot pass first-year algebra are unable to succeed in a college-level major based on advanced math and science, and therefore are not invited to participate in the senior-high MESA.

Students in the academic track, with support and encouragement, continue to the next level of college-prep courses. With each success, they usually enroll in the course that follows.

Student preferences deserve respect. Someone interested in art, journalism, or law will probably bypass calculus, chemistry, and physics in college. So MESA advisors invite the ones whose career interests, hobbies, and favorite courses relate to math or science.

From the beginning, MESA inspired a team effort at Tech. Beth Cobb and Somerville recruited UC Berkeley students as MESA tutors. They also interviewed students to identify their college goals and career interests. Students received advice on choosing a college and help with the college application process. As a result, MESA graduates enrolled in colleges with majors they had hardly dared dream about only a few years before.

Rodney Maxwell, a Tech senior then, remembers meeting UC physics professor Harry Morrison, one of the few black professors in the sciences, and other university faculty on MESA's first campus field trip.

"They gave us reinforcement," says Maxwell. A MESA participant for only three months, Maxwell still recalls its influence on him choosing engineering as a career.

UC Recruitment Not the Goal

Although UC-sponsored, MESA is not a UC recruitment program.

"We expected and encouraged students to enroll in any college that interested them and for which they could qualify," Smith says. "This continues as the philosophy of MESA program sponsors on each MESA college and university campus in California."

Dr. Crystal Darling opted for UC Berkeley. "In high school I knew I wanted to go into science, but I didn't really have a direction as to what area."

Students aiming for college sometimes felt like outsiders, she says. "Some of the other kids thought you were a little peculiar, but in MESA we had that moral support among us."

Darling majored in chemistry for three years and did a year of graduate work in secondary education with the idea of teaching math and science. She caught the teaching bug by tutoring Berkeley High students. But now she's teaching neuroradiology, following a switch to medicine. She's a staff member of Children's Memorial Hospital at Northwestern University.

MESA students participated in the Math Department's regular after-school study sessions two afternoons each week. Teachers encouraged them to work with each other and with tutors provided by MESA. Math students dropped in for help on their homework, taking advantage of earlier invitations. When necessary, students who had enrolled in advanced math classes, whether or not they were MESA students, could earn extra money by tutoring younger students.

Another alumnus who tutors is Brandon Hewitt. He's vice president of Khafra Engineering Consultants with offices in Louisville, Birmingham, and Atlanta.

"We do presentations about engineering in the school. We do a lot of community work, and I still tutor. What do I tell them? That they have to have good study habits, study consistently and that college was hard, but do-able."

Birmingham, which is Hewitt's headquarters, offers a program exactly like

MESA's, including cash incentives for good grades. "I wanted that money when I was in school, so I made sure I got those grades," he says with a chuckle. "I don't know if I would even have bothered going to a lot of those classes if it wasn't for the program."

His firm employed forty-three people in 1992, making it one of the largest consulting engineering companies in the southeast made up of African Americans. It handles wastewater treatment plant and airport design for government agencies.

During MESA's first years, Somerton, using his industry contacts, scheduled field trips that put students in touch with the engineering and scientific work cor-

A science experiment

porate America conducts. In addition, the high schoolers profited from contacts with university students and adults outside the high school environment. MESA participants learned companies needed them and promised opportunities for them after they earned degrees.

Field trips gave students an inside look at how the corporate world functions, how engineers, mathematicians, and scientists perform their jobs, and some advantages and disadvantages of working in industry.

"We went to Shell Oil on one of our trips," says Steve Flournoy, who joined Oakland Tech MESA program in 1972. "They had a blackjack computer game—and I owe Shell a lot of money. Trips like that were a big benefit. I hadn't had much exposure as far as what colleges and corporations were about. I ended up becoming more and more interested in computer science because of our field trips."

Flournoy has spoken at MESA banquets, tutored, helped on MESA Days, and served on the organization's state board and the San Jose Center's Industrial Advisory Board.

"Without MESA, I don't think I would have made it to college," he says. "People like Mary Perry Smith and Professor Somerton were instrumental in encouraging me. They were there also during those college years. I needed that. What MESA's doing for a lot of young kids is giving them that feeling of knowing they can try and they can do. They come from the same streets, the same schools, and they're now successful."

Oakland Tech faculty who taught students math and science not only took turns monitoring after-school study sessions, they accepted offers from Smith to supervise some field trips as well. They also enjoyed a rare opportunity to talk one-on-one with industry people and see modern technical equipment in use.

"Teachers often got more out of these trips than the students," Smith says.

Somerton solicited summer jobs for students, making an important differ-ence in their lives. Most had never worked and lacked know-how on fitting into a technical work force. They learned practical, scientific concepts that shed light on and clarified classroom tasks and discussions. Some kept those jobs through-out their college years; a few even stayed with their firms after graduation.

Early MESA students themselves were invited to help develop and refine the program. Student representatives brought their ideas and aired grievances before the Steering Committee.

"Your contributions to this process are important," Somerville emphasized at the outset.

He held regular sessions with students, soliciting their suggestions and, from the beginning, making them feel MESA was their program.

Mary Perry Smith

The Mellowed Mary Perry Smith

Born in Evansville, Indiana, the eldest daughter and one of six children of the Rev. Henry Allen Perry and Anna Whittaker, young Mary Perry seemed destined for the role of teacher. Her father was an African Methodist Episcopal minister and a teacher. Her mother also taught. Other relatives were teachers as well. But Mary dreamed of becoming a doctor or an engineer and hoped to attend Purdue.

"My older brothers took chemistry, physics, algebra, geometry, and trig in high school," she says. "Since textbooks were handed down to the younger children, I took those courses, too. Even though I was a girl, it was expected of me because I was in the college-prep track."

She won a state scholarship entitling her to attend any university or college in the state.

"My father discouraged me in studying to be a doctor or an engineer," she says. "He said it would be difficult for a black woman to find a job in any field but teaching."

Rev. Perry prevailed and she ended up at his alma mater, Ball State, a teacher's college. She majored in math and science, however, and graduated in three years. Sure enough, as he'd predicted, she couldn't find a job in Indiana teaching in her field. Even a master's degree from Purdue didn't help.

She moved to Houston, accepting a teaching job at Texas Southern University. There she met her husband-to-be, Norvel Smith, who had found no job opportunities in Philadelphia despite B.S. and M.S. degrees from the University of Pennsylvania.

"If we're going to continue teaching in college we need doctorates," they decided after their marriage.

They moved to California and enrolled in UC Berkeley, where he completed his doctorate. Mary Perry Smith took the national teachers' exam with a score high enough to assure her of a job. She began her teaching career at James

Denman Junior High School in San Francisco.

"I loved teaching science in particular because the students were so interested in it," she says. "The sputnik era helped."

She occasionally had outside help too.

"Right in the middle of a class I was teaching—a geology session about earthquakes—we had a major earthquake in San Francisco," she recalls.

In 1961 she became a math teacher at Oakland Technical High School. She describes herself then as a "hard-line" teacher. Students who neglected their homework or scored poorly on tests received D's and F's.

"And I gave a lot of D's and F's," she admits. "Students questioned this approach, saying, 'You're just too hard on us. You need to take more time and sit down and talk to us.'"

She mellowed, but kept her standards high.

"Students need someone who pays attention to them and encourages them, saying, 'You can do it,' and sticks with them all the way through," she says. "They don't need people who come in and say, 'Rah, rah,' 'Just say no,' 'I am somebody,' and other meaningless slogans. They need people who say, 'If this is where you want to go, then I will stay with you and help you learn the things you need to know to get there.'"

This philosophy is the heart and soul of MESA, according to teachers who serve as MESA advisors.

Smith was distressed when African-American students who did well in geometry rarely followed through with the advanced math courses required for college calculus. She searched for ways of pointing them toward not only advanced math but also the chemistry and physics needed for technical and science programs in college. David Stonerod, Tech's math department head and a creative teacher, introduced computers at an early date and she climbed aboard the bandwagon.

"David was one of those nerds who is always out there doing crazy, fun things with mathematics," she says.

This progressive approach led MESA's founders to select Tech as its first school and Smith as its first school advisor.

Her experiences made her the logical choice for MESA's first director of programs at the Lawrence Hall of Science, headquarters of the MESA Statewide program, from 1977 until her retirement in 1982. She remains active as a member of the MESA Statewide board of directors. Her community volunteer work includes a leadership role for the Black Film Makers Hall of Fame, which she helped create.

What are her greatest satisfactions?

"Sometimes, reading in the paper about current MESA students graduating from high school and being awarded scholarships," Smith says. "Other reports about MESA students studying engineering at prestigious universities. While I was teaching, seeing MESA students attending UC Berkeley return to tutor other students at Tech. The camaraderie that exists among MESA students and how they take pride in themselves and pride in their peers in the program."

Teachers tell her that if it weren't for MESA they would have given up teaching a long time ago. Pride of the parents in their children's achievement is another source of satisfaction for Smith. When their students excel, parents think she is a super human being. In her usual manner, she credits MESA, rather than herself, for giving their children the opportunity to achieve their potential.

Chapter 4
Involvement Sparks Ideas and Support

MESA's first grant of $15,000 came from the Van Loben Sels Foundation based in San Francisco and established by an industrialist interested in improving educational opportunities for minorities. Bill Somerville, then executive director of The Wright Institute in Berkeley, paid the bills and handled the paperwork out of his office.

"What we need is a permanent home," said Harry Morrison, a UC Berkeley physics professor, at a MESA Steering Committee meeting for the fledgling program. "The ideal place for MESA is at the Hall."

The "Hall" was the Lawrence Hall of Science perched high in the hills above the campus. Named for Nobel Laureate physicist Ernest Orlando Lawrence, who joined UCB in 1928 and developed the cyclotron, the Hall serves as a science education research center. It focuses on improving pre-college science teaching. The Hall's innovative science and math teaching programs are known around the world.

"It's the perfect spot," agreed Alan Portis, a physics professor who was director of the Hall.

The steering committee's unanimous vote led to a move in September 1971. The Hall continues today as MESA's official sponsor and handles its personnel and financial matters. Professor Marion Diamond, director of the Hall since 1989, serves as the MESA program's principal investigator. The university's College of Engineering became a co-sponsor and remains heavily involved to this day. Wilbur "Bill" Somerton, a professor of engineering, agreed to serve as the first faculty advisor.

Also on the original steering committee: UCB professors Gil Corcos and

*MESA
Students at
1991
leadership
conference*

—Photo by John
Jernegan

David Gale; Oakland Technical High School teachers Mary Perry Smith and
David Stonerod and principal Bill Miller; Somerville; and Ben Fraticelli, a
minister for the Christian Churches (Disciples of Christ) and a minority rights
activist.

The church and its regional office, the Christian Churches of Northern
California and Nevada, pitched in with a donation of $1,500 at a crucial point late
in 1970 after the initial grant was spent. "The church's grant prevented the
program's collapse," says Somerville. He applied for another grant from the Van
Loben Sels Foundation. It reviewed the program's potential and approved another
$15,000. The money enabled MESA to continue and funded its important
scholarship component.

Somerton, Somerville, Smith, and Portis joined the first MESA Advisory
Board, which also included four industrialists. The board set policy and served
as the governing agency.

Beth Cobb, assistant dean of Admissions at Mills College in Oakland, served
as MESA's first director. She became Beth Cobb O'Neal in 1975, and now is the
associate director and vice president of the Law School Admissions Council in
Pennsylvania. She likens the council to the College Boards.

From the outset Smith, Oakland Tech advanced math teacher, served as the
first high school faculty advisor. She took over many of the functions of Cobb after
Cobb returned to foundation work in 1971. Smith made a major contribution to
MESA by establishing the high standards of performance required of students to

this day. In her status report at the September 1971 MESA Advisory Board meeting she recommended that ninth grade students, who begin the math sequence with algebra I, should be included in the program. Oakland Tech started at tenth grade, so she invited its main feeder school, Woodrow Wilson Junior High, to participate. It joined the program in 1972; Zelma Martin became the MESA advisor in the first expansion of the program. Ninth graders were encouraged to join. Martin interviewed, counseled, and tutored them. "Continue your math and science studies in high school," she kept repeating.

Early Expansion

"We can attract additional funding by extending MESA to other schools in the area," Somerville told the Advisory Board. With the board's go-ahead, he met with Smith and Somerton to establish criteria for selecting new schools, then rank eligible high schools on this basis. They agreed on these main requirements:

> The target population (African-Americans, Mexican-Americans, Native-Americans and Puerto Ricans) constitutes a majority of the student enrollment.
> The school possesses a strong math/science program.
> The school boasts capable, dedicated teachers and counselors with the interest of all their students at heart.
> The school administration fully supports MESA and gives its advisor at least one period of release time to work with MESA students.

John F. Kennedy High in Richmond became the second high school in the MESA program during 1973. Math teacher Elois Irvin, who easily fulfilled the "capable, dedicated" and other requirements, became the advisor and in 1992 was still filling that role, making her the dean of MESA advisors in California.

"When MESA came to JFK, the student body was nearly fifty percent African-American," Irvin says. "The rest were white, Chinese, Japanese, and a few Latinos. There were three black students in math analysis, one in calculus, about nine in geometry, four or five in algebra II, and between twelve and fifteen in algebra I. The total school enrollment was nearly 2,000. MESA highlighted these disparities and greatly increased the number of minority students in college-prep math and science. It gave the faculty a very positive attitude.

"A truly dedicated school advisory board supported the program. The members included industry and business representatives, people from government and the school, as well as parents. They didn't just advise; people like Gene Neblett from the Federal Power Commission and George Coover with General Electric arranged field trips and helped with day-to-day management. At our meetings, it was interesting, even funny, to see executives with offices large enough so they could prop their feet on their desks try to sit comfortably in cramped spaces in straight-backed chairs."

After Kennedy High School's principal signed MESA's formal agreement, Barrett Avenue Christian Church in Richmond hosted a banquet for the students and their parents, teachers, and school officials. Members of MESA's advisory board also came. Dressed in their finest, the youngsters basked in the limelight as the guests of honor.

Banquets, over the years, proved effective as a means of informing people, honoring students and generating enthusiasm. The first awards banquet at the Lawrence Hall of Science attracted seventy-two people. Local Christian churches hosted some welcoming and year-end awards banquets. Before long, commercial banquet halls were needed for the growing number of students in the program. Local businesses and organizations paid most of the bills.

MESA hired Kevin Canada as a part-time coordinator of the Oakland Technical High and Woodrow Wilson Junior High programs. This gave Smith time to assist with the Kennedy High start-up.

The First Marks

After three years of successful operation, the MESA Advisory Board requested an outside evaluation. Educational Analyst Cecil T. Shaw was hired to interview MESA students and graduates, review records and the results of a questionnaire filled out by the 1973 MESA students. He reported:

> ...The MESA program is in the process of meeting its major goals and objectives. Most MESA students who have already graduated from high school are presently enrolled in college and are majoring in the areas stressed by the MESA program. Ninety percent of former MESA students have entered college. All of these students presently enrolled in the MESA program intend to go on to college; 89 percent of these students will be majoring in mathematics, science, engineering or related technical fields. These results are encouraging, for they indicate that many students of minority background are entering college and preparing themselves for occupations where few individuals of Black, Chicano and Native-American background are employed.
>
> Students enthusiastically support the MESA program and the kinds of experiences they have had because of the program. Most students expressed total support for the activities contained within the five components of the program—tutorials, counseling, field trips, scholarship incentives, and summer employment. Students generally appreciated the comprehensive nature of the experiences they had, especially as they relate to academic needs.

Shaw recommended:

1. More student input and involvement.
2. Devoting more time to students' individual needs.
3. A clearer definition of the student selection procedure.
4. Program expansion in the Bay Area and throughout the state.
5. The addition of more staff to assure smooth running of all components
   of the program.

MESA implemented all of the recommendations. Shaw's report also opened the door for additional funding. Joseph Frisch, associate dean of the College of Engineering at Berkeley, had become an ardent supporter of MESA. He used the report findings at a General Electric Foundation meeting promoting increased numbers of minorities in engineering and science. Then he recapped the report for a National Academy of Engineering meeting in Washington, D.C. in May 1973. The Alfred P. Sloan Foundation soon granted MESA $25,000, making it possible to add Berkeley High School, including its ninth grade students. By 1975 smaller donations from General Electric Foundation, Exxon USA Foundation, Union Oil Foundation, and Bechtel, Inc. aided in this expansion effort.

Berkeley High, helped by a federal demonstration project grant, split the school into twenty-four interest units. An "On Target School" dealt with students interested in math, physics, and electronics under the direction of Robert Rice, who also headed the school's career center.

"The career center became the hub of the MESA program where its students met during lunch hours for discussion and tutoring," says Rice, the school's first MESA faculty advisor. "Students considered tutorials to be the most important part of the program, with incentive schol-  arships running a close second. Tutoring was done mostly by advanced Berkeley High students, many of them in MESA, but advanced students received tutoring from UC Berkeley student volunteers.

"Problems of elitism arose, and stu-

MESA students studying design problems

dents who were not in the program criticized the 'special' treatment MESA students received. These problems were not completely solved but were subdued when some of the athletic stars in the school were admitted to the program," Rice recalls.

Capable, dedicated faculty advisors like Murphy Taylor and Evelyn Lawton began steering students toward rewarding careers. The frequent turnover of advisors, however, at times kept Berkeley High from achieving the continuity Smith and Irvin brought to Oakland Tech and Kennedy High.

Annual Report Debuts

In 1974, Ron Grossman was hired as director to coordinate the UC Berkeley MESA Center's programs for the four schools. His first annual report for 1975-76 showed 170 students fairly evenly divided among the three high schools. Out of thirty-three who graduated during 1975, thirty-one enrolled in universities and colleges. Twenty-one of the enrollees opted for math-based fields of study. In addition to the Alfred P. Sloan Foundation, three industry foundations, and two companies had provided financial support. The report mentioned the first summer enrichment program, conducted by the Lawrence Hall of Science, for a group of thirty-five MESA students.

A Turning Point

Dr. Percy Pierre, an active proponent of improving the access of minority students to careers in science and technology, visited UC Berkeley. It was near the end of his 1973-75 leave from Howard University where he was dean of the School of Engineering. His assignment: advise the Alfred P. Sloan Foundation on the feasibility of a national effort to increase opportunities for minorities in engineering. Smith, Professor Harry Morrison, and Associate Dean Joe Frisch hosted Pierre's visit. His introduction to MESA led to additional Sloan Foundation funding and his assessment of the program would bring major increases of donations in the future.

"Compared to other professions, engineering has done a remarkable job of educating minorities," he said upon returning to the Berkeley campus as a Regents' Lecturer in 1991. "The Mathematics, Engineering, Science Achievement program is an example of one of the nation's outstanding pre-engineering programs. In fifteen years we've doubled the percentages (of minority graduates) from 3 percent to over 6 percent in 1988, but it is not enough."

In the fall of 1976, Smith and Somerton were "accosted," as they put it, by Theodore Lobman, program officer for the William and Flora Hewlett Foundation. John May, executive director of the foundation, had hired Lobman as a consultant earlier that year to find why so few minorities became engineers, and what the foundation could do about it.

"For six months I reviewed the limited available literature, especially the Sloan Foundation report, and visited many university campuses, including UC Berkeley's MESA," Lobman says. "...Later that year I presented the report to the Hewlett board. It indicated the major components of the Sloan Commission strategy: scholarships for minority engineering students, high school level curriculum, a consortium of universities aiming to increase the number of masters' level minority engineers, and so on. My report argued that the most important problem, and the least well attended so far, was building the pool of minority students interested in and prepared for college-level engineering. The Hewlett board decided to concentrate on that problem and to emphasize California. Naturally, we started with MESA."

Lobman proposed to the MESA board, and in particular to Smith and Somerton, that MESA expand throughout California. A substantial grant by the Hewlett and Sloan foundations would fund the growth.

"We're concerned that a rapid, broad expansion might deteriorate the program's high quality," Smith told Lobman.

Somerton added, "We've all worked hard to achieve that quality. It's built in. It turns out that new talent at the new centers enhances the program's quality. It's an outstanding example of synergy at work."

The Consortium Approach

"Consider your community resources," said Lobman. "You have public schools, engineering colleges, employers of engineers, educational professionals, professional engineering associations, college student groups, and associations of parents and community leaders. These constitute a consortium. The public schools and engineering colleges could be your focal points, but crucial to MESA's success would be industry's guidance, support and cooperation.

"Your challenge is the complexity of the beast," Lobman continued. "Take the availability of high school courses leading to engineering course work, as just one example. Alone, these courses would give incomplete preparation for most minority students without exposure to the engineering work place or minority role models. That's why I'm recommending the consortium approach. It can serve as a catalyst for the general improvement of schools. You can imagine the curriculum, counseling and recruitment advantages of linking a high school to engineering colleges. Another point: Your local program will invite local contributions, and you'll need these foundation fund supplements."

Lobman's rationale proved prescient. Efforts to improve secondary education soon escalated, especially for minorities. Most of these efforts, plagued by piecemeal, short-term strictures, faded from the scene. Lobman saw that industry and other philanthropic efforts could be channeled through a consortium.

Lobman, Smith and Somerton clustered for a long discussion. Lobman assured them the founding group would continue in full charge of the program and quality control would be the major priority. The two foundations agreed to support the program for five years. This would provide MESA with the continuity needed to track the progress of students long enough to see if the program achieved its objectives. Another reason favoring expansion came when the Sloan Foundation indicated its support would end unless the program expanded. An impelling reason indeed.

Smith and Somerton recommended and the MESA board approved the statewide expansion. The first Hewlett-Sloan grant was used to inform college and university engineering departments about the program and assess their interest in establishing centers, staffed by MESA, with the aim of serving local high schools.

Elois Irvin:
"It's Like Icing on the Cake"

"I grew up in a totally segregated south when teachers were actively involved in the students' lives," says Elois Irvin. "My all time favorite teacher,

Onie Nelson, taught fifth and sixth grades. She took me home with her on some weekends and encouraged me to do well. I went shopping with her and played the old piano at her place."

Influences like this made Irvin an ideal advisor when MESA arrived at John F. Kennedy High School in Richmond, California in 1973.

"When I started teaching here it was disappointing to see so few blacks in math classes. After MESA, enrollment in college prep courses increased. Not many students knew about engineering."

Her slogan became "The earlier the better" for MESA signups. "Ninth and tenth graders tend to stay with the pro-

Elois Irvin

gram and nearly all of them go on to college. Some of the older students are overcommitted to sports, jobs, or activities."

Other teachers noted the time Irvin devoted to the cause and said, "You must be crazy. You're not even getting paid for this."

Irvin, however, still finds it fulfilling, something that needs to be done. "As I saw more kids who enrolled in my courses go on to the university, then come back, it made it worthwhile. It's a rewarding experience; like the icing on the cake."

Parents of MESA students urge younger children—their own and the neighbors'—to participate. Teachers help spot kids with potential. MESA students recruit their friends. These efforts attract many new students each year. In a move that altered its demographics, the school began attracting more Caucasians in 1992 presenting a possibility for MESA-like programs for them.

"Teachers look to MESA students for leadership," Irvin says. "They (the students) know what's required of them; they've set goals. The principals have high expectations for the program, and they recognize its value, but they don't really step out. There's not a lot for them to do. Maybe we're too efficient," she adds with a laugh.

Each year she thinks that this might be the time when MESA isn't needed any longer, then, "I become convinced the opposite is happening; the need hasn't decreased at all."

When she recalls parents in the program, she thinks of George Harris, a retired oil company technician, who still serves the high school PTA even though all four of his children have graduated. Michael Harris is studying marine biology at UCLA. Coretta is an engineer in Los Angeles and helps as a mentor and a tutor for high school students. George, Jr. is a computer science major at the University of California, Berkeley, and is married. Zachary's majoring in engineering at Stanford and tutors in his spare time at the MESA center nearby.

MESA students acquire a new dimension from summer academies, Irvin says. "They get a lot out of it. Parents wield an influence on this decision. They let their children know the value of a long range goal and that sometimes you must sacrifice for it.

"A lot of parents didn't emphasize education when I was young. Children were needed on the farm. But mother was always their advocate. She took those parents to task and persuaded some of them to keep their children in school."

Irvin graduated from Morris Brown College in Atlanta and first taught in a segregated school where children received a strong inculcation of values—a facet of education that didn't survive after desegregation.

"I've heard teachers say, 'When I'm down and feeling low, I go to MESA.' There's promise and something new."

Irvin, a single mother of four, serves as the Sunday school superintendent at her church in Berkeley where she tutors each Wednesday and helps operate its singles ministry. She also serves in leadership roles for Delta Sigma Theta, a sorority with a heritage of more than 200 years of community service.

Madeleine Fish:
Making the Complicated
Understandable

When they hollered, "Hi, Ma. Hi, Pa," students of Grant High School in Sacramento were showing a blend of respect and affection toward MESA Advisors Madeleine Fish and Brian Suki.

"Brian and I were a math and science teaching team, and our MESA students were part of the family," says Fish. "If we took a field trip, we stopped for pizza on the way back. They knew the type of behavior expected of them, and that's how they acted."

Those reactions had not always been typical. When the native New Yorker began teaching at Grant High in 1964, only 2 percent of California schools counted more students with families receiving AFDC than Grant High. That also was the year the University of California, Berkeley's graduating class of 1964 included only 30 underrepresented minority students, she recalls.

MESA arrived at Grant High in 1977. Five high schools in the Sacramento MESA center signed up 125 students, but administrative problems threatened the program. MESA advisors from the five schools arranged a rescue operation. They banded together to operate the program themselves after the original director was released. By the end of 1991 the number of MESA students had grown to 3,100.

"People in the schools feel an ownership of the MESA program," Fish says. "It also spills over. When we increased the math, science and physics sections, this extended to other classes and activities. MESA is there every day. Many other programs amount to just putting a finger in the dike."

If a group of MESA students filled half the bus for a visit to an industrial plant, "We filled the other

Madeleine Fish

half with students from other classes." If a teacher learned a MESA student was thinking about dropping physics, the reaction was, "Whoa. Wait a minute. Go see Fish first." Invariably, Ma Fish persuaded the youngster to stick with it.

She didn't experience comparable support herself while attending school in Manhattan.

"The schools in New York City lacked a feeling of community," she recalls. "Teachers didn't take a personal interest. My high school didn't include anyone I'd gone to junior high with. It was filled with strangers."

When her sister, Lucy, bogged down in physics before a regents exam, Madeleine dashed to the rescue. Her coaching led to a test score above 90.

"I discovered I could make the complicated understandable," Madeleine Fish says. And the discovery eventually led to a career in teaching, helped by New York State University's new Stony Brook campus faculty that almost out-numbered the students in the first years.

"It was an incredible educational experience. The school didn't have an education department as such, but if anyone wanted a teaching credential they obligingly would switch a regular course number to an education number. I thought, 'Well, a teaching credential might be nice to have.'"

She served as class valedictorian, obtained a degree in biology and a graduate degree in chemistry from Brandeis University. When her husband, Richard, joined the California State University, Sacramento faculty in 1964, she began teaching at Grant High. She led classes in physics, chemistry, and biol-ogy her first full year and learned, "That's not the way to live."

"It took me about five years to get away from the idea that the material was the key to teaching. Then I began to enjoy the students, began shaping their attitudes toward school and each other, and began establishing personal relationships."

The home-like atmosphere of her classes developed mutual respect. No one experienced embarrassment from criticism before others. By the end of the first year, students knew certain behavior was expected. No one was sent out for discipline.

"Teaching got to be fun," Fish says.

It continued that way for 22 years when she accepted the California State University, Sacramento director's post for the MESA Minority Engineering Pro-gram, which the university underwrites. Fish also directs a Project Success pro-gram in which both large and small employers put beginning students on the payroll for intermittent work as they attend school on a five year schedule.

Native American display at central California MESA Day at UC Santa Barbara

Chapter 5
Grow—Or Else

By early 1977, plans called for expanding MESA from a pilot program to a full-fledged California effort aimed at making an impact on African-American, Mexican-American, American-Indian, and Puerto Rican students preparing for science, engineering, and related careers. Both the Sloan Foundation and the commission that had produced the catalytic *Minorities in Engineering: A Blueprint for Action* report in 1974 rated secondary school preparation programs and minority networking as top priorities.

California's role appeared crucial. The state contained high percentages of minority students, and forecasts indicated even higher ratios in elementary and secondary schools increasing as the 21st Century neared. The state boasts a large number of public and private engineering schools. Thus in the late Seventies it could claim an integrated educational system, with the exception of attracting minorities into technical fields of study, despite the efforts of active minority engineering societies. It was a time when aerospace, computer, electronic, and high-tech construction industries needed engineers and scientists.

"As a separate nation, California is the world's eighth largest economic force," Governor Jerry Brown kept telling voters.

Clearly, unless minority participation in science and engineering could succeed in California, efforts elsewhere, even if successful, would lack the impact that success in California would have.

Storm Clouds Hover

Some potentially inhibiting trends existed. Only minor rumblings surfaced about the inability of public schools to educate students. Schools with high ratios of African-American and Mexican-American students sent few graduates to universities and colleges. When they did, only a handful were prepared to pursue a mathematics-based field of study. So a crisis that by 1987 would affect schools throughout the country, already had shortchanged California minority students. In addition, the Bakke case raised questions. Allen Bakke, a white engineer, alleged the University of California at Davis School of Medicine denied him a place in medical school by selecting a less qualified minority student. The courts ruled in his favor and it threatened the varied educational programs aimed at minorities. Finally, a tax revolt was also in full swing. Opponents of Proposition 13 claimed its severe restriction of property tax dollars would cut services by public agencies, including schools.

These storm clouds kept MESA's founders from waxing too enthusiastic about the future, despite California's many favorable characteristics.

Bill Somerton and Mary Perry Smith still worried about the potential effects of too rapid an expansion on quality of the program. The commitment of multi-year funding by the Hewlett and Sloan foundations eased this considerably.

The die was cast. MESA's new Expansion Steering Committee first developed an administrative plan that would guide the development of MESA programs in California. The MESA Coordinating Agency (later to become MESA Statewide) evolved and was headed by a project director (a UC Berkeley faculty member), MESA's Board of Directors, an Executive Committee, an executive director, and a support staff.

Conference Provides an Overview

Somerton and Smith visited several universities and colleges with MESA center potential, distributing booklets and describing the expansion. They also promoted an upcoming MESA Expansion Conference/Workshop. More than 100 persons representing sixteen universities attended the April 16, 1977 session. Each contingent included not only deans, administrators and faculty, but also high school teachers and their district administrators, plus representatives from area industry, business and government. Prominent foundation and minority organization representatives also attended. One of them, Robert Finnell, deputy director of the Committee on Minorities in Engineering, served as keynote speaker. Later he would become the first MESA Statewide executive director.

The daylong conference/workshop provided an overview of the problem of attracting minority group students into math-based fields. Delegates learned about MESA's beginning years, helped by a special booklet explaining the expansion process. Members of the Expansion Steering Committee and MESA's Advisory Board led small group discussions. Robert F. Content, assistant director of the Lawrence Hall of Science, with help from other steering committee members, described guidelines for MESA center proposals in the closing session.

Fourteen of the sixteen universities submitted proposals; ten were funded for start-up operation that year. Three more university centers embarked in 1978-79 and the full complement of fifteen centers was reached during the third year of the statewide move. The number of students served increased from 170 before expansion to 881 the first year afterward and in the fifth year, to nearly 3,000. In 1992, the junior and senior high participants exceeded 11,000 in California.

"Bob Finnell's leadership over the first six years of the expanded program was, without a doubt, responsible for its unqualified suc-

Mary Perry Smith and Bob Finnell   —Photo by John Jernegan

cess," says Somerton. "His organizational ability, penchant for quality through training, and his tracking system to assess the success of the program—all these things were instrumental in developing enthusiastic support for the program from foundations, industry, the California State Department of Education, and the State Legislature."

Finnell established his priorities when he took on the MESA executive director's assignment in July 1977. They included:

Setting up MESA Statewide's office at the Lawrence Hall of Science.
Designing governing boards in a way that would achieve long term goals.
Writing detailed plans for the program's expansion.
Establishing a data base that tracked performance of students and each of
        the ten new MESA centers.
Devising training programs for staff members and volunteers.
Expanding public relations programs to reach larger and specific audiences.
Looking for sources of additional funding that could sustain the program
        beyond the five years funded by the Hewlett and Sloan foundations.

"Success in meeting these goals helped establish MESA's credibility in high schools and universities," Finnell says. "It also set the stage for the sustained effort we needed to influence rates of secondary school graduates and their subsequent performance at the university level."

Programs rated top priority also. Smith, a seasoned Oakland Technical High School math teacher and MESA's first advisor, was selected to be the first statewide program director. She helped implement the MESA model at each new center by training MESA directors and advisors. She established activities that supplemented basic aspects of the program as described in the next chapter.

Except for the people involved in MESA outreach or faculty of engineering schools contacted by Somerton, MESA was not widely known throughout California in 1977.

"Our challenge was to replicate a tested program in ten urban or rural centers to build a solid base within five years," says Finnell. "This would give MESA impetus for growth over several decades while equipping minority high school graduates with course requirements and motivation to pursue degrees in science, engineering, or related fields of study."

What would attract junior and senior high students to an academically oriented program that stimulated and stretched their intellectual capacities? For years many minority students heard a message, "You don't measure up," either directly or by implication.

"Unless MESA's image and substance attracts adolescent minority students it will fail, no matter how well funded or how strongly the leadership believes students can succeed," Finnell said.

The Concern about Ownership

Another concern guided MESA's program. "Local school administrators, teachers, parents and volunteers should see MESA as their program," Finnell said. "Otherwise, they may not feel responsible for its success in their territories."

A decade of federal and state programs, by the mid-Seventies, had left high school teachers and students skeptical, cynical or at least resigned about outside efforts to improve their schools. They saw programs arrive in September with fanfare, and watched them disappear with nary a word by June.

"We'll structure the program so that each local MESA center feels responsible for its direction," Finnell said. "Otherwise, teachers and administrators could view it as being owned by somebody else and therefore not their responsibility. And it will fail."

MESA also faced the challenge of establishing credibility among the university, foundation, corporate, and governmental agency worlds. Their decisions could open doors, facilitate growth, and bring in new sources of funding. Some universities already operated outreach programs for minority students. "Why," they argued, "start a new program when we can do the job?" The job they did, however, lacked MESA's math-science academic preparation component, staff expertise, and its multi-year focus. Many university programs only dealt with identifying students or motivation that enhanced self-image.

A Need for TLC

Harvey Mudd College in Claremont, California, unsuccessfully tried a Program of Specially Directed Studies, bringing underrepresented minority students in with special tutoring and a modified course load. "We wanted to see if we could get them to mesh with the intense, highly competitive Harvey Mudd program," says Thomas T. Woodson, retired engineering professor and chairman of the college's Department of Engineering. "It may have lacked the TLC."

Woodson, utilizing twenty years of experience with General Electric and six years with UCLA, specialized in generic engineering design. In 1977 when he sought help on a project involving a minority group, the GE Foundation told him about MESA. He contacted five area high schools, applied for a MESA grant and helped hire Nancy Eddy who in turn signed up about sixty-five students.

Throughout the state, educators, executives, and government administrators had seen ineffectual programs come and go. So, crucial to MESA's expansion was establishing credibility for the program with media, institutional committees, forums and conferences. Also, visibility could be achieved by involving leaders from around California in governing MESA.

Following the April 1977 expansion conference, engineering schools in California began working on proposals for the MESA Statewide Office. MESA's single center at UC Berkeley then worked with 170 students on a $35,000 budget. The original five-year expansion goal: to have fifteen centers by 1983. Each year they would serve 3,000 students and produce about 700 graduates. Each center would work with from one to four high schools and expand operations once it took root. Funds from the initial Hewlett-Sloan grant would pay for staff salaries, student services, and other costs. In-kind contributions from local universities, school districts, professional societies, and companies were anticipated.

In July 1977 MESA occupied an office on the second floor of the Lawrence Hall of Science. Finnell and Smith shared a small office with secretary Virginia Thompson. For the next year the cramped office served as the nerve center for MESA's expansion.

Marketing efforts focused on MESA as an academic skills building program rather than one aimed at just identifying qualified students or motivating students to pursue studies in science and engineering. The message was clear. To interest and prepare more underrepresented minorities for math-based fields, MESA would focus on these areas:

1. Provide academic support services to MESA students, helping them acquire the necessary credits and grades to enroll in university engineering or math-related fields.
2. Provide career exploration activities in math- and science-related professions.
3. Provide opportunities for men and women from industry, universities, engineering societies and government science-related agencies to work with MESA targeted students in math, science, and engineering professions.
4. Establish educational enrichment activities that prepare minorities for engineering and related careers.

MESA's focus was based on some key assumptions. One was an attempt to come to grips with the central issue raised in the Constitution and in the civil rights movement: How best to use the talent of the nation's citizens, particularly members of groups virtually excluded from this country's decision-making power centers?

Minorities worked in social agencies, education, churches, and other fields on the periphery of decision-making and power strongholds. MESA's goal of opening doors for professional management or technical careers aimed at serving the best interests of underrepresented students as well as the schools, professions, and the social and economic interests of the nation.

Secondly, MESA assumed its initial target should be students from underrepresented groups in junior and senior high enrolled in college preparatory math, laboratory science, and advanced English classes. Then, later on, the focus could be broadened to university and elementary schools.

Third, MESA centers would be located near high schools with significant percentages of underrepresented minority students not enrolled in math, science, and English courses, and where the principal and teachers supported MESA's goals. In addition, need for the program would be linked with the potential for success. Many programs in the Sixties and Seventies began when a need became apparent, but they failed for the lack of the right courses, teachers or resources. No one had realistically gauged the potential for achieving results.

Fourth, MESA assumed 3 to 4 percent of the underrepresented minority students were potential MESA students and graduates. This conservative estimate was based on what happened to white students at high schools with adequate math and science programs. Over the years, the 4 percent ratio proved about right.

Fifth, MESA assumed three years was the minimum time needed to produce graduates from one of the new centers, and assure students of its support during that time. This contrasted with some quickie delivery programs that essentially "creamed" existing students, creating an illusion of success. They failed by

*Students
in the
laboratory*

—Photo by
Pamela E.
Clarke

forgetting education is a step-by-step, sequential process.

Sixth, MESA assumed core funding for a MESA center would attract additional resources because no one else was effectively addressing the technical interests of California's major institutions. The expectations included in-kind educational enrichment services from local industry, professional societies, and other local organizations; volunteers to interact with students on career choices, pathways to success, and one-on-one dialogues; and, finally, funds from local sources.

The Driving Force

These assumptions behind MESA's expansion rested on the key premise, an article of belief among everyone involved and the force driving the entire effort— **minority students could excel**. They could be stimulated to enroll in and complete advanced math, laboratory science, and English courses with the help of tutoring, counseling, field trips, speakers, summer enrichment programs and incentive grants. Others held widely differing assumptions. Some felt any investment would be tossing money into the wind because minority students lacked interest and the capacity of pursuing math and science successfully. Others felt that merely enrolling students in the right courses would produce academic success. Some felt students should be left to their own devices; the sink or swim philosophy. MESA saw opportunities for success while others saw insoluble problems.

As MESA's effort grew, technically educated minority talent grew more important in a changing global environment and in the U.S. where complex challenges required human know-how and copious resources.

MESA's approach concentrated on preparation rather than remedial methods. It made maximum use of existing school resources, particularly teachers, instead of setting up a parallel system. It pre-selected students interested in science and engineering rather than working with all students. MESA's flexibility permitted local centers to add or modify activities, making them attractive and effective in each particular environment. It concentrated only on the schools with potential for improved student performance. It emphasized day-to-day academic preparation for university programs in engineering, science, and related fields, in contrast with vocational educational programs or one-shot activities that reached students once a year. Finally, MESA recognized that a well educated high school student gains the option for a variety of career paths, and that science and engineering provided an excellent background for non-engineering careers such as medicine, business and management of public and private institutions and agencies. The MESA model proved attractive because it hit a responsive note: work with previously passed over students achieved a constructive result and benefited all.

MESA operated under the University of California at Berkeley with lines of reporting through the Lawrence Hall of Science director and the Chancellor of UC Berkeley, but a Board of Directors guided it. During the expansion year an Industry Advisory Board and center directors helped harness the resources of industry, universities and other institutions.

Staff members of corporations and professional organizations joined the MESA team. Among those providing guidance: Bechtel Corporation's Richard Collins and Bruce Thiel, Northrup's Jaime Oaxaca, TRW's Paul Jackson, The Los Angeles Council of Black Professional Engineers' Benito Sinclair and Al Richardson, and the Society of Hispanic Engineers' Gilbert Herrerra.

Statewide Office Roles

The MESA office from the 1977 start-up of the California expansion has taken the program statewide from the pilot center at UC Berkeley, handling the planning, evaluating, and managing aspects. Later, when New Mexico, Colorado, Washington, and other states expressed interest, the MESA office played a key role in programs there.

Five years after MESA's statewide expansion, its annual budget was just over $1 million, an amount that equalled the figure the Sloan-Hewlett foundations estimated would be spent over five years. From 1977-78 to 1981-82, MESA raised $3.5 million. The funding helped launch a university level program that complemented its high school base.

Five-Year Plan			
No. of Centers	Students	High Schools	Graduates
1977-78	1	170	3	-
1981-82	15	3,000	60	700
'82 Actual	15	2,519	102	785

Using demographic and secondary school enrollment data, MESA developed a long term expansion plan. Carried out in cooperation with Dr. Rex Fortune and Dr. Ed Bispo at the California State Department of Education, the planning also involved people at the systemwide offices of the University of California where Drs. Alice Cox, Floyd Weintraub, and Frank Collea shared information. At the California State University system, Drs. Stephanie Adams and Esteban Soriano also worked on phases of MESA planning.

The California Office of Postsecondary Education's Dr. Pat Callan, Bruce Hamlett, and their colleagues have shared their studies and program projections over the years. Members of the California Assembly John Vasconcellos, Peter Chacon, and Teresa Hughes, and Senator Gary Hart played crucial roles in funding the statewide expansion of MESA.

"With updates from these quarters, MESA could modify plans and activities, showing how its quality education program reinforced academic objectives that students, parents, and others found beneficial," Finnell says.

Robert Finnell
Rides the Wave of the Future

When he suffered a severe heart attack in 1986, Robert Finnell characteristically opted for unusual treatment.

"I loved good food and seldom exercised," he says. "After a lot of research, I concluded bypass surgery, the usual procedure then, was not for me."

His study had revealed an alternative based on lifestyle changes. He decided to give the program a try. It required a diet of no more than 10 percent fat, yoga, stretching and breathing exercises, meditation, and plenty of sleep.

"My coronary function has improved, I feel better, and my general health has greatly improved," he says.

The *Reader's Digest* featured Finnell in a February, 1991, article about the program and he participated in an episode of a 1992 "Nova" PBS television show on the subject.

When he became the first executive director of the MESA Statewide program in 1977, his hard work and dedication to the cause should have raised warning flags, but his healthy appearance and optimistic outlook aroused feelings more of envy than concern.

Finnell started school in the Forties in Laredo, Texas. After three years he headed across the border for a bilingual school in Mexico. He attended junior high in McAllen, Texas, and attended the high school there where his mother taught Spanish. Although the community was 98 percent Mexican-American, Anglos made up nearly half of the small high school's enrollment. And Anglos held all the key positions in the school.

"In my first five years in that community I was the only person whose family had both Mexican-American and Anglo parents," he says. "It didn't take long to see who moved ahead and who didn't in American society."

After attending Baylor University and the University of Texas and reading literature and history, Finnell taught at the University of Pennsylvania, then the University of Texas.

"It soon became clear I was furthering the education of only an elite group, so I decided I wanted to connect with the communities I had grown up with," he recalls.

He ran an East Austin housing development corporation for low-income persons, mostly African-Americans and Mexican-Americans. But he missed the field of education and went back for a year's study on bilingual education.

"I realized minority communities would never acquire power unless they broke out of their traditional fields, which at that time were mostly menial labor," he says. "Those few who were professionals worked in the non-power areas of education, theology or social work. I decided minorities must be prepared to enter the professions of engineering, the various sciences, higher education, and business and organizational management."

While working in Washington, D.C. as a consultant in bilingual

Robert Finnell

education, Finnell learned of a committee forming at the National Academy of Science. It became known as the Council on Minorities in Engineering. With his background in education, business, planning, and management, plus an intense interest in the goals of the committee, he joined the effort in 1974. One of the committee members, Dr. Percy Pierre, Dean of Engineering at Howard University, was a Sloan Foundation consultant looking into formation of a secondary school network that could develop programs aimed at preparing more minority students for careers in engineering and science. Pierre identified Mathematics, Engineering, Science Achievement as a possible program that could meet the needs of such a network and encouraged Finnell to look into it. Finnell attended a MESA board meeting and kept track of the program. In 1977 he was invited to give the keynote speech at a MESA Statewide expansion conference. Several pre-college programs around the country were addressing the problem, but Finnell concluded they lacked MESA's roots in the community and its ties with teachers, industry, and universities. When offered the position of executive director and the challenge of expanding MESA around the state, he opted for this unparalleled opportunity to further its cause.

As the program expanded, he visited high school teachers, students and principals. He attended board meetings at various new MESA centers and participated in interviews for their directors. He took field trips, attended MESA Days, and feasted at four or five year-end awards banquets. His leadership and management skills gained the respect and confidence of everyone involved.

He started activities that improved the program and assured its longevity. Teacher training sessions, for example, gave MESA teachers new ways of dealing with problems they faced daily in connecting with their students. He initiated a data collection system that documented the program's progress in reaching its objectives. This documentation helped expand industry's role as financial contributor, equipment donor, volunteer supplier, and cheerleader. The data also convinced state legislators that MESA, the wave of the future, deserved substantial financial support.

These activities took Finnell away from frequent direct contact with persons in the field carrying out the program. He repeatedly acknowledged their importance, however, by insisting on broad ownership of the program. He encouraged new ideas. Many of them still color the fabric of the basic program.

"People at all levels take pride in ownership of our program because of Bob's leadership and the dedication he inspired in all who worked on it then," says one MESA veteran.

Finnell's resignation as MESA's executive director in 1983 shocked his coworkers. He accepted the prestigious position as president of the National Action Council for Minorities in Engineering, which he served with zeal until his heart attack in 1986.

Tomas Arciniega

Tomas Arciniega and the Viability Factor

Amid a severe budget crunch and the recent approval to initiate a School of Engineering at California State University, Bakersfield, Dr. Tomas Arciniega may at times consider himself wedged between the proverbial rock and a hard place. The university's president says Bakersfield is underserved as far as engineering education is concerned. Major oil and gas industries and important agribusiness in the area need engineers. The university's pre-engineering program and a community college link could phase into a full- fledged engineering school. In addition, a large minority population, served by one of the largest MESA programs in the state could provide capable and well-prepared students. With such a need and such an opportunity, Arciniega continues his quest, despite a dollar drought, for a School of Engineering program which, in itself, can make a significant contribution to the state's economy. Arciniega has been an active member of the MESA Statewide Board of Directors since the early 1980s. As a strong supporter, he is also realistic.

"I'm not convinced we started something so completely new it was like a bolt of lightning that inspired us and here we are. It's not so sacrosanct it should be replicated exactly and all schools should genuflect at this altar. I don't believe that at all. I do believe the basic elements of what makes the program successful are reflected in the MESA model. It sets high expectations for students, then enables these students, through careful staging and enabling kinds of activities, to achieve those expectations. Our commitment to support these students well beyond their immediate needs is a key to success of the program."

Arciniega grew up in a low-income federal housing project in El Paso, Texas, in a predominantly Spanish-speaking environment.

"There was not a whole hell of a lot different about me," he says in answer to a question about people or events that influenced him. "I think it was a combination of factors and a lot of luck. Of course there were teachers, parents and my family, all of whom were supportive along the way. Although my folks did not have any extensive experience in education and neither was a college graduate, there was always a willingness to be supportive and an expectation it was possible to succeed, and they were there to help.

"In the housing project, the people on one side of the canal were black and on the other side were Latinos of Mexican background. The schools in El Paso did not desegregate until I was about to graduate. The terrific thing about growing up in that neighborhood was that it was in the shadow of a branch library. This kid gravitated and took to the library, becoming involved from second grade on in all of the special reading programs they had. I can remember the days when it was really a big deal to be able to travel downtown to the Carnegie Library. Interestingly, some years later I became a trustee of the Carnegie Corporation."

Arciniega received his B.S. in Education at New Mexico State University in Las Cruces and his M.A. and Ph.D. in Educational Administration at the University of New Mexico. He taught at the University of Texas, El Paso before moving into the California State University system, first at San Diego, then at Fresno. He was selected from 120 candidates for his present position as president of CSU Bakersfield. Arciniega is regarded as an expert in the areas of educational programming and bicultural education.

As a member of the MESA board, he recognizes his role as overseeing the administration and management of the program, assessing its progress, and looking into sources and expenditure of money. Most important, he believes, is coming together as a board with the executive director and staff in developing a sound strategy to keep the program not only moving but growing as well.

"I would say that, without exception, the board members and people who become board members do so because they are convinced of the importance and viability of the MESA model," Arciniega says. "We must find ways to convince people at various levels—state government, foundations and industry—that the program should be funded at a level that allows it to continue to do what it's been doing so well and also fund the expansion and the new directions that periodically evolve out of the core program. MESA has a success story to tell and it's crucial to be telling it over and over again."

Don Gillott:
A Formula for Sound Sleep

"When I first came to Sacramento in 1968, and even before that in Pittsburgh, I was concerned about underrepresented women and minorities in engineering. It seemed if you spotted anything but a white male in class, something was wrong."

This concern proved a boon for California State University, Sacramento back then because it kept Don Gillott, the new head of the Electrical Engineering Department, receptive to ideas for change.

"I began working with some Hispanic friends," he recalls. "We developed a program to bring Hispanic children to the campus. They visited labs and classes, talked with students so they could see some opportunities in the field of science. It was called the Chicanito Science program. It was the first of its kind, and it opened the door for MESA at CSUS."

The MESA program had gone statewide in 1977 and CSUS was one of the first universities invited to participate. UC Davis also ranked as a top contender but could not be chosen.

"You're too close to CSUS," Dean John Kemper was told.

Don Gillott, who had moved up to dean of CSUS's College of Engineering in 1978, wasted no time embracing the MESA concept and signed up first.

"How about a joint center?" Gillot asked Kemper. They worked out the details and Sacramento's Central MESA Center became, and still is, the only center sponsored by two universities.

The offer is characteristic of Gillott. His MESA associates describe the restless dean as a man willing to go to bat for them, a supporter with an upbeat attitude.

Don Gillott

A native of Latrobe, Pennsylvania, he earned his B.S., master's and Ph.D. in electrical engineering from the University of Pittsburgh. He escapes the halls of ivy whenever possible, seeking to emulate another Latrobe native, Arnie Palmer.

Gillott's proclivity for quick, decisive action surfaces in some challenges affecting students. When the American Electronics Association formed a Sacramento chapter in 1988, Gillott agreed to head the education committee.

"We started a program to improve the math and science education of children, and modeled it on the MESA plan," he says. It operates in schools with fewer underrepresented minorities than MESA requires.

Industry's role is a big factor in the success of MESA and its techniques to help students while they're in college. Another program, inspired by MESA and supported by Pacific Telesis, is MEGA, which encourages underrepresented minorities to enter and continue in graduate school.

"You can see it's an entire package," Gillott says. "In 1992, MESA began training teachers at the first grade and kindergarten levels, and its influence will extend through high school. The MESA Minority Engineering Program sustains this effort through college and helps in job placement. MEGA will carry this process on into graduate school."

Only a few MESA-related challenges have confronted Gillott.

"You'll always find certain people who may feel threatened by change," he says. "Some people questioned our use of resources for MESA's targeted group. For example, I okayed a 24-hour a day study hall right next to Engineering, despite some pressure for additional classrooms for all students."

Gillott says that the university's officials look at MESA as its most successful minority program, yet they still channel resources into other programs best known for faltering or failing.

"We should at least take advantage of the ones proving successful," he says.

MESA, for the most part, isn't creating problems.

"It's a program that lets me sleep at night. It's the other things that keep me awake."

Karl Pister:
Creating Long-Enough Ladders

After words of thanks for the invitation and praise for the high school honorees, Karl Pister told students at the first MESA banquet in 1973, "The MESA program is like a ladder. If you have to work on the roof of your house, you must have a ladder that's long enough to get you up on the roof."

An engineering professor then at the University of California, Berkeley, who

Karl Pister   —Photo by Don Harris

became chancellor at UC Santa Cruz in 1991, Pister also said, "In your careers and your lives, if you want to reach a certain goal, you've got to build a ladder that's long enough to reach it. The MESA program is designed to help you build that long-enough ladder."

After he became dean of the College of Engineering at UC Berkeley in 1980, he helped the Berkeley MESA Center develop outreach ranging from middle schools through the graduate level. This included a university level MESA Minority Engineering Program network and the appointment of a dean who guided the development of the Berkeley engineering program in this area. "MESA was the core of it," Pister says. Efforts like these earned him in 1987 the Vincent Bendix Award for Minorities in Engineering, the field's most prestigious honor for educators involved with minorities.

A Stockton, California native, Pister, received a B.S. degree with honors and an M.S. in civil engineering at UC Berkeley, then completed graduate studies at the University of Illinois for a Ph.D. in Theoretical Applied Mechanics in 1952, the same year he returned to UC Berkeley as an assistant professor.

"Cabrillo Community College, next door to us here at Santa Cruz, is receiving support to start a MESA center," Pister says. "There is a heavy concentration of Hispanic high school students in the Watsonville/Salinas area and a large African-American community in Seaside. We don't have enough outreach to these communities yet, so I'm looking forward to developing the program here."

Can MESA make a difference in other parts of the country?

"The MESA program model is an excellent one," says Pister (rhymes with "feaster"). "It's easily portable. In fact, fifteen states have MESA or MESA-like programs. The main thing you need is leadership; someone must take responsibility. Then you need a good staff, one that understands young minority students. You need people who are sensitive to their concerns, comfortable in minority communities, and know how to relate to people. They must have lots of energy and be willing to work hard.

"If you're going to sustain any kind of success you've got to get a commitment from the faculty to see this is a vital part of the academic program."

Pister became chairman of the National Research Council's Board on Engineering Education when it was created in 1992.

A decade has passed since *A Nation at Risk* warned of the deterioration of America's K-12 education system. "Despite much hand-wringing, very modest progress has been made since then to remedy the situation," he says. He suggests that universities become more involved with the "pipeline" that begins in kindergarten and ends with the production of practicing engineers. "We need to enrich the quantity, composition, and quality of the pipeline's flow."

Improved communication among educators in secondary schools, community colleges, state colleges, and universities could improve the pipeline flow of well-prepared students, Pister adds.

—Photo by John Jernegan

Elementary MESA Day activities in Sacramento

Chapter 6
Organizing for Success

The MESA Statewide Office serves as the hub of a wheel around which the rest of the program revolves. The wheel spokes contain frequently used communication lines from each MESA center into the Berkeley office and back to the centers. Since each center also communicates regularly with other centers, this communication is the rim of the wheel. An engineer might say it is, more aptly, a thirty-two-sided polygon with all diagonals drawn. The Statewide Office would then be the center of the sphere generated from these diagonals.

An executive director heads the MESA Statewide staff with responsibility for operating the program in a manner consistent with its guidelines and for seeing that centers receive adequate funding. The executive director's staff of 13 professional and clerical workers provides day-to-day support services, training, and leadership for center staffs. A statewide advisory board (MESA Board) is made up of leaders from industry, education, and government, and advises MESA on a wide range of policy matters. Chairs of the Board over the years are listed in Appendix I.

The Statewide MESA Office functions include providing each center's staff support and services through:

In-service, orientation and staff improvement activities.
Leadership in developing policies that maintain the program's thrust.
Maintaining and developing a stable, growing funding base.
Developing major industry support through an Industry Advisory Board.
Encouraging political, educational and community support through the
    involvement of Board of Directors members.
Conducting statewide and regional meetings, in-service and orientation

sessions for staff, student participants, parents and advisors.

Developing and maintaining a statewide data base on participants.

Promoting MESA at university systemwide offices, major corporations and state and national legislative hearings and related organization meetings.

The MESA Statewide Office also oversees the advisors' workshops and program evaluation.

A Statewide program director provides in-service training for staff and MESA advisors—the teachers who volunteer their time to work with MESA students. Once a teacher commits to implementing the MESA concept, the program often becomes institutionalized at her or his school and practically maintains itself. Center directors may change, and their experience and ability may vary, but MESA activities continue at quality levels in schools with committed teachers.

Advisors' workshops exemplify successful aspects of the program by:

Letting teachers know MESA appreciates their work of supporting and encouraging students.

Allowing teachers with common interests and training to share successful methods. Most of them teach math and science at secondary schools, but they also include some counselors and English teachers who work as part of each school's MESA support team.

Providing opportunities to learn about successful teaching techniques and materials related to math and science education. Elementary school teachers also participate in several hands-on science and math workshops.

Enabling teachers to learn from and rub elbows with leading scientists and engineers.

Reinforcing the purpose of MESA and implementing its program at each school level, elementary through senior high.

Advisors who attend MESA workshops return to their schools enthused and reinvigorated. The original workshop took place in May 1978, the first year MESA expanded statewide. The advisors' workshop expenses, including travel, came from industry and participating school district funds, solicited by MESA, a practice that continues today.

The first workshop gave the Statewide staff a chance to evaluate the program's effectiveness. Teachers who attended appreciated the rare opportunity of meeting with their peers, having other professionals hear and value their ideas. They also learned new concepts and techniques from professionals in the math and scientific fields. Several advisors who attended that first workshop still worked with MESA in 1993, fifteen years later.

These first participants asked for future workshops in August, reasoning this date would give MESA activities a terrific kick-off for the school year and improve the relevance of the orientation of new advisors by experienced advisors. An August session generated enthusiasm that could persist through the year-end MESA banquet, the experienced advisors felt. They were right.

Evaluation activities proved important. Some educational programs measure participation of students served, but, from the first, MESA focused on who completed courses, who completed high school with three or four years of math, science and English, plus an interest in pursuing a math-based field of study, and who actually went on to matriculate in those fields in college. MESA also gathered and evaluated data on the program activities at each center and the students' participation in them. Miguel Trujillo, Daniel Ulibarri, and Richard Santee were among MESA staff members who designed the data base system. Thus MESA built into its operations a data base outsiders and staff could use for evaluations. It proved valuable when UCLA's Center for Evaluation assessed MESA's work in 1982.

The MESA Center

A MESA center, based in an engineering program on a college or university campus, issues a clear message that here is a prestigious academic program instead of a remedial program for the economically disadvantaged. The original design called for a senior, tenured engineering faculty member to be the Faculty Sponsor at each MESA center. This proved an asset to the program and sparked industry's support.

Guidelines for establishing new MESA centers included proposed review criteria and, among other things, accounting program implementation and data collection procedures. Bob Content and Barbara Baker of the Lawrence Hall of Science and Gus Manza at UC Berkeley's Office of Research, helped draft and review the contracts and other documents needed to establish a center. The procedures, plus the evaluations, showed center directors their funding depended on performance. It was not something they could take for granted. Many outreach programs provided automatic funding and their built-in constituencies influenced the way funds were allocated. MESA, on the other hand, operated on private grants and evaluated center performance on the basis of results. This immediately told others a different set of players with a different set of values had entered the arena.

As a result, a degree of tension built up between MESA centers and parallel programs and other interest groups that began to recognize a new set of ground rules might govern minority student programs. Rather than encapsulating itself with like-minded institutional employees, MESA actually diversified its team,

MESA tutors at a leadership conference —Photo by John Jernegan

creating a cross section of individuals from industry, education, and the community who reviewed its progress. This predated the cooperative efforts between industry and education much touted in the late Eighties.

The MESA faculty sponsor assumes fiscal responsibility for MESA grants, hires and monitors the center director and holds the ultimate responsibility for operating the MESA program at the center. The center director handles the day-to-day running of a center while the faculty sponsor contacts superintendents, school board members, industries, and some school-site principals, particularly when a school or district first learns of the program. A faculty sponsor also selects and directs the center Advisory Board and participates in center activities involving students, parents, and school personnel.

The center director is assisted by a part or full-time assistant and clerical staff, depending on the number of students served by the center. The Statewide Office funds the staff and center programs. The director provides support services needed by advisors and students, maintains a data base and statistics on the center's students, and works with the faculty sponsor, schools, community, parents, and industry, promoting the goals and objectives of MESA.

The center director provides the main link between the Statewide Office and the local community and university. He or she determines the success of the center program. Just being energetic, intelligent, and interested will not guarantee success, but all directors need these qualities. School system experience gives a director a head start on program activities at each MESA school site.

Center directors must build coalitions among teachers from different MESA schools as well as between schools and industry and the university. They supplement their budgets by writing grant proposals, working with parents and industry representatives on fund-raising activities and creatively soliciting and using in-kind assistance. One important skill a center director needs is how to work effectively with volunteers. MESA advisors, school site principals, faculty sponsors, industry speakers and tutors, and parents volunteer their time to make a MESA program work. In some centers these helpers outnumber paid staff many times over.

An Advisory Board supports and promotes the MESA center. It is made up of representatives from local businesses and industries, the community, and the university or college. A dynamic board assists the director with fund raising, getting school board support, and deciding which schools can be provided MESA's services. Board members also assist with:

1. Establishing policy on the number of students' field trips. Too many trips interfere with school work; too few limit students' chances of developing a broad range of career choices.
2. Researching and soliciting a wide range of interesting field trips.
3. Deciding on the best ways to involve local industry.
4. Discovering creative ways to reward outstanding efforts and achievements of MESA students.

Each local advisory board advises and assists the faculty sponsor and center director in adapting statewide policies and programs to local needs and conditions, providing they're compatible with statewide goals and objectives.

"Before I started working here I'd always had 'do-gooder' jobs," says Patricia Souza, part-time director of MESA's small center serving Santa Rosa, Healdsburg and Ukiah. "This is the first time Republicans ever liked me. They're really glad about what we're doing. This is a satellite, part of the Sacramento center, because we have no university in the area."

Some parents of her MESA students don't appreciate the value of a college education, especially for their daughters. Some parents are illegal aliens who didn't hear about the amnesty program or chose to ignore it. Despite the challenges, she's upbeat. "Everyone tells me, 'You're doing a great job.' Everyone likes me."

The MESA High School

Once administrative approval for a program is given, the right person within the school must be found; otherwise, nothing of substance happens. Advisors and co-advisors form a team that becomes the foundation on which successful MESA programs grow. They open channels of communication between students and the outside resources MESA provides.

That contact person becomes the MESA advisor. This teacher must support the concept of working with MESA-targeted students and know which courses they must complete for success in college in a math-based major. Additionally, the advisor identifies the teachers known for stimulating and challenging students. This person must know required internal school procedures for enrolling students in the proper classes and be on good terms with the decision makers, who can hinder or speed the progress of a program such as MESA. Since the goals of MESA relate to the students' improved performances in math and science, it follows, then, that math and science teachers, the persons who work within the institution, know the subjects and know the students enrolled in them. They hold the keys to successful MESA programs.

MESA is a teacher-oriented program because its premise rests on the concept that good teachers already go the extra mile, giving interested students assistance and encouragement. Too often, however, these same teachers find themselves overcommitted. MESA gives them extra hands and resources, helping them challenge and support the interests of some of their students. This support also helps these teachers work more effectively with all of their students.

Advisors become the day-by-day available friend, consultant, teacher, tutor, and standard-setter for MESA students. They help students select the right courses and see that they succeed by scheduling study sessions and teaching study skills. They gather students together for meetings where students support each other's interests, develop leadership skills, and learn more about math and science professions and college requirements. MESA advisors play roles like teachers who nurture the talents of their gifted students in football, basketball, or drama. This is the model MESA advisors follow, and it raises the question: Why don't more academic teachers do for students what high school coaches do for students who play sports?

MESA Students

The student selection process garners MESA's close attention. This helps emphasize the importance of selecting young people who can best benefit from the services the program offers. Advisors need a clear understanding of which students the MESA program targets. They must also realize only a few senior high or university students will choose careers requiring a college major in mathematics, science, or engineering. This percentage varies greatly, depending on the high school's academic standing. The growing interest in math, science, and computers, nationally, will undoubtedly influence how this percentage grows in the future.

MESA is not a recruitment program for science and math-based careers. Instead, it nurtures science and math **interests** which students already possess. At the elementary and middle school levels, MESA activities involve a larger percentage of the students enrolled in those grades. These students receive information about math and science; they develop their natural talents and interests in these areas through hands-on activities. MESA advisors help these younger students succeed in the appropriate classes by developing their study skills.

MESA advisors at the senior high level select and work with algebra or geometry students, ones already on their way toward achieving career goals in math and science. MESA must focus its limited resources on helping students achieve success in their academic math and science courses. Advisors must also make sure these students stay on track, avoiding courses that do not lead toward careers that interest them. If MESA makes its participants successful graduates, then they themselves become the recruiters and catalysts for stimulating other young people.

By creating a greater demand for math and science classes, MESA encourages schools to offer more advanced courses in these areas. For example, in 1985 the Woodrow Wilson High School in East Los Angeles had barely enough students to fill one chemistry class. In 1992, with MESA solidly in place, five chemistry classes exist. At another school, an advanced math class was nearly canceled for lack of students. After MESA arrived, two classes were packed.

Results like these are critical in high schools with high African-American and Mexican-American enrollments. By working with these students and their parents, MESA develops a peer group within a school community that supports high academic performance. They make it okay to be good students. This is especially so since MESA students receive a wide range of awards and special recognition, including cash awards.

MESA parents play an important role in determining the success of any high school MESA program. The MESA staff informs parents of the goals, purposes, and activities of the program and involves them in many events. Students whose parents participate persist in greater numbers with MESA and achieve higher academic standards.

Jim Harold:
Backed by District Dollars

After a rocky start, the Capitol MESA Center in Sacramento rates as the largest center in the entire MESA network and is unique in several respects.

"We've got one of the finest supportive deans that you can find," says Jim Harold, center director, in explaining its success. "Even when he can't support us financially, we can always count on the other kind of support."

His reference is to Don Gillott, Dean of the College of Engineering at California State University, Sacramento, a strong supporter of MESA since its state-wide expansion in 1977.

"As a counselor at Sacramento's Kennedy High, I had a desk with a phone on it," recalls Harold. "So that's why I became a MESA center director."

Harold is a Bottineau, North Dakota native whose parents couldn't afford to send him to kindergarten. His mother, an ex-teacher and a college graduate, helped him prepare for first grade.

"I kept winning the top student award and the prize was taking Friday afternoon off, which seemed a bit of an anomaly." Harold came under the influence of some caring La Porte High School teachers and, "I still know them." The family had moved to Northern Indiana during World War II. One of his teachers advised him to try Manchester College after Northwestern University's tuition proved out of reach. After three years, he transferred to the University of Southern California and graduated with a degree in English and French.

A hitch in the Air Force revealed the importance of what he now urges MESA students to consider: "Make sure you take your required math and science courses so you can have some options."

After a transfer to Sacramento in 1955, then an Air Force discharge, Harold married and began teaching at McClatchey High.

"I saw so many kids needing help, I started training to become a counselor," he says. Eighteen months later he became the first counselor assigned in the district based on credentials. He joined MESA in 1980, taking over as director of a troubled center program.

The uniqueness of the center lies in Harold's success in obtaining school district funding, which amounted to $150,000 in 1991, half of his total budget for that year. School district funding has a long history at the Capitol MESA Center. Mary Perry Smith was instrumental in setting up a MESA program in the San Juan School District even though none of the nine schools met MESA's target population enrollment requirements. The district, anxious to have a MESA program, regrouped students from its schools so a sufficiently large number of targeted students was available. The district also agreed to provide financial support of the program. MESA students there now meet as a group once a week in the evenings. Hewlett-Packard volunteers tutor them several nights a week. "It works," Harold says. "It's one of our largest programs. I think you just have to fit the model to the circumstances."

This triggered additional financial support. It's now required from all of the eight districts in the Capitol MESA Center area.

"We really made sure that a school bought into the program before we would even serve it," he says. "I think now we are talking about ownership of the program. Superintendents, even in this year (1992) of financial crisis, have set the MESA budget apart. It cannot be bargained away and thus I do not expect a decrease in school district support in this difficult economic year."

It was not always this way. "If school district people don't understand MESA, we have to educate them," Harold says. Support comes from people like Ron Morgan, former Kennedy High principal. The feisty Morgan, after moving up to a district administrative post, was at a meeting of school district officials. When the subject of MESA funding arose, so did Morgan. He argued for increased funding, declaring, "MESA is the only program that did what it said it would do."

A spinoff from the San Juan experience has been the funding by local industries of programs in other schools that do not meet the target population or other MESA requirements. IBM supports a program at Sacramento City Elementary School by providing tutoring and other services. The American Electronics Association sponsors MESA-like programs in Sacramento schools without a target population. In working with MESA, industry has learned how to focus funds and resources effectively.

"Now other industries, instead of just calling themselves sponsors, look at investing money in program sites that are either underfunded or in elementary schools, which are not included in the MESA network," says Harold, who was one of the first winners of the Wilbur H. Somerton Award given for outstanding center leadership.

Harold finds MESA is not always regarded as a panacea. Some people are actually opposed to it. Some school principals, for instance, see MESA as a threat to their autonomy. They consider that school funding going into MESA is a loss from their budgets. That's where the leverage power of MESA and direct industry funding to the school comes into play. Harold generally can convince skeptics that the loss of a MESA program will deprive the entire school of teaching materials and in-service activities MESA provides. For example, MESA advisors are taught how to use Full Option Science System kits in the MESA summer institute. After consumable stocks are replenished, MESA advisors allow other teachers and students to use these kits.

Another unique feature Harold instituted is small stipends for all 105 school advisors. He reasoned that teachers who also coached sports earned extra pay. He campaigned so, for the first time, academic teachers received compensation for the extra hours spent on MESA. In a sense, this helped justify the financial support school districts provided for the MESA program.

"We started at the lowest level—the amount that a volleyball coach could earn a semester," Harold says. "In addition, teachers are excused from classes for MESA work and MESA-sponsored meetings. In those meetings, teachers are treated as professionals in the same way business treats clients or consultants. That professional treatment gives teachers the spark to develop innovative programs."

Richard Alvidrez   —Photo by John Jernegan

Richard Alvidrez: "It was Like This Was Made for Me"

When Richard Alvidrez became MESA center director at California State University, Los Angeles, he encountered unexpected resistance in expanding the program in the East Los Angeles area.

"I was convinced kids were capable of a lot more than was expected of them. Most of the students in the area were of minority groups. Asians represented about 5 or 10 percent of the total enrollment, but 90 percent of the students in advanced math and science classes were Asian," Alvidrez says. School administrators did not view the absence of other minorities as a problem, and even those who did shrugged their shoulders and said, "Yeah, it's a shame." Both reactions troubled him.

Were there frustrations in starting new school programs?

"Some we anticipated, some we didn't, and the ones we didn't we just couldn't believe people would resist us so stubbornly. We could not understand why there was such a stake in seeing so many kids reach so much lower destinies than they were capable of. Why? It made no sense. Kids who could have gone to professional schools were counseled to go to a state college. Kids who could go on to a four-year school were counseled into junior college. Kids who could have gone into a technical occupation were barely finishing high school."

Once the program started, MESA advisors, following tradition, took part of the load off the counselors by counseling their MESA students.

Why would schools and school districts resist taking on another program?

"The situation with schools is that they see programs come and go all the time. We show up with a lot of enthusiasm, saying MESA is the greatest thing since sliced bread. Finally they say, 'Oh, okay. Sure, we'll be in the program. Sure, why not? Here are our commitments to it.' The commitments may turn out to be one-sided, like unrequited love. But as time went by and we kept in there year after year, we saw their expressions change, 'Well, yeah, they're still here,' was the reaction, and they would look at MESA differently. They began realizing there were bottlenecks in their own programs, and MESA was showing them the way out."

Some schools balked at focusing on MESA's target population.

"People tried playing hardball with us on this issue saying, 'Well, if you can't let everyone in the program, you can't have it here.' We said, 'Fine.' And we bypassed schools that gave us that kind of resistance. Sometimes there was a change of heart, or more likely a change in principal, and the word would come, 'Bring in the program.'

"Teachers receive MESA very well because of the achievements of MESA students. If you can find a way for kids to show high achievement, you've got to beat off the teachers who will follow you. Some kids may have bad vibes and MESA teachers will try to minimize that by saying, for example, 'We recognize your problem, but last year you were absent from your math class eight times and you brought it down to two times this year. You can do it! We have a study group for tutoring after school today. I want you there and I don't care about your basketball or drill team.'"

Asked about parental involvement, an important program facet in some centers, Alvidrez says, "We had good involvement from the parents of students who were doing well. All of our kids at the top of the class had parents who would come to our meetings, so we said, 'We think these kids are successful because their parents are behind them and, somehow, that happened without us. Let's take an indifferent parent and exert the influence that creates a student who will be successful.' We tried, but we never found a way to do that. It appears that up to the fifth or sixth grade, parents have a lot to do with their children's education. After that, the kids follow their group and, apparently, parents give up on them."

In a survey of MESA seniors in the CSU LA center, students were asked, "Who was most influential in your decision to go into math and science?" The number one person was their math or science teacher. Taking a clue from this, center staff decided to use surrogate parents for those students with indifferent parents. An outstanding example of this is the wife and husband MESA advisor team at Woodrow Wilson High School in East Los Angeles. Evelyn and Domingo Torres-Rangel, math and computer science teachers, were joint recipients of the MESA Mary Perry Smith Award. It is made annually to pre-college school advisors who exhibit outstanding leadership and service for MESA students.

"They were really mom and dad to many of their MESA students and the kids related to them," says Alvidrez. "They had a refrigerator and a couch in their classroom, making it attractive for kids to hang around. They thought they were home. Great numbers of kids enrolled in math and science courses, reversing a trend we saw at the school. Those teachers were leaders for the other advisors and an inspiration for the rest of us," reports Alvidrez.

Alvidrez, who served the California State University, Los Angeles, MESA center for ten years, won one of the first Wilbur H. Somerton Awards. It goes annually to a pre-college center director who exhibits outstanding leadership with the MESA program. He left the center in 1990 and joined the staff of the Jet Propulsion Laboratory at California Institute of Technology.

His original training was in engineering, but he received a second degree in math and did graduate work at CSU LA. He grew restive in his engineering career, wanting something more people-oriented. He tried his hand at teaching but an ineffectual school situation disenchanted him. He recalls his reaction when he heard about an opening for a MESA center director:

"This is something I have been waiting for. This is so great. So many people have not been paying attention to a large part of the population and it was way overdue. It was like, my God, this was made for me."

Asked what he would like to see MESA do in the future, Alvidrez says, without hesitation, "I think MESA ought to start doing things boldly. We should introduce more science for kids at the early ages—pre-school, kindergarten, first and second grades. You go out and talk to kids and you find every kid wants to be something. We need to invest more money in achievement, for we will get it back. If we don't we'll pay for it anyway. Recent reports show it costs more to send a kid to jail than it costs a kid to go to Harvard. It's like making money for the country when we invest in kids. There's no payback for the kids who go to jail. But the kids who go to Harvard, or any other first-class school, will more than pay back the cost of quality education in terms of what they put back into the economy in the way of expenditures for goods and services and the taxes they pay."

It's clear Alvidrez puts back into the economy not only his outlays for goods, services, and taxes, but also for those students he helped. Even though he left MESA as a working participant, he remains a part of the family in his active, outspoken support.

Victor Cary:
"I See Myself as a Manager"

Typical of MESA people, Victor Cary, director of the UC Berkeley MESA Centers, says, "I love to talk about the program. I could rattle on forever. I love the work we do. The product is sound and the technology is sound. I'm always amazed at the beautiful simplicity, yet effectiveness, of the MESA model and the fact it is not static, that you can be very creative."

The original and oldest MESA center in the state, the Berkeley center boasts a tradition of excellence that continues under Cary, who was appointed director in 1987. Because of the flexibility allowed by the model, no "typical" MESA center exits. Cary's particular program strengths include summer programs, Saturday Academy, parental involvement, and fund raising.

Victor Cary
—Photo by John Jernegan

"I've been in education for twenty years. My first experience was that of a high school instructor in Richmond," Cary says. "It was a great experience but also a great frustration because of the limitations in the structure of schooling as it existed then, and now. I was looking for a way to provide my services in a way I thought could produce better results. So I got into early academic outreach program. I've worked in many of them including Upward Bound, Partnership Program, Educational Guidance (a federally based program), and a talent search program. When the opportunity for MESA came along, I applied for it and won the position of director.

"The thing that interested me about MESA was its history, its solid background, but more importantly, its focus. The more I got involved with understanding how the model was set up and the vision of the model, particularly around the networking focus, the more I was really sold on it. In my earlier work with educators I found they tended to be in an education network and not really in network with the community to the extent they should be, and certainly they don't network with industry, as MESA does. The dynamics of this networking provides an extremely powerful mechanism to accomplish the work we do."

What does a center director do?

"It's sort of like being the ringmaster of a circus, but really, a director is an educational entrepreneur," Cary says, "an educational broker who provides a conduit for the different segments of society with an interest in the issues of educational equity and serving students of color in a way that makes a difference. I try to bring together those various segments—the university, public schools, the community, industry and parents—in a way that makes some kind of sense.

"Originally, the MESA director was a person who inspired the kids and the teachers at the schools. We still do that—I have an assistant who visits the schools. But as the program gets larger (600 to 700 students) you can't have the personalized touch you might have had when the centers were a lot smaller. I really see myself as a manager, more along the corporate lines in a way. Often I wear coat and tie because I must make convincing presentations, generating more resources as the program grows in size and quality. Acquiring and managing always limited funds more creatively occupies about 50 percent of my time."

From the standpoint of program elements, Cary reports, "Our center was responsible for updating the data-based management system for improving the tracking of our kids. It's used statewide now. Another innovation, the independent student program, evolved because of the tremendous demand for our services. Students who don't go to our target schools can participate in some of our program activities. A number of students in our Saturday Academy who come from parochial and private schools are our target constituency but not our targeted schools. We charge a fee for students from independent schools to attend our programs. We give plenty of scholarships if families can't afford to pay the fees. I never deny a child participation because of the money.

"I am proud of our Summer Academies. This summer (1992) we have 135 students in our Young Scholars program (pre-high school students) and 160 students in our Pre-College Academy. We begin the program planning and development in October for the following summer.

"In addition to the outstanding teaching staff to run the academies and the after-school enrichment programs, I now have a person on my staff who mobilizes and organizes parental involvement in the program. Providing an organizational structure, I find, is one of the most crucial things you must have in order to involve parents and volunteers. In other words, you say, 'This is your organization. This is what we need you to do. This is how we do it. This is where we need you.' We need to be very specific. 'On this day, at this time, we need you to do this.' It's worked like a charm. We're now taking this model to the schools, trying to organize parent groups at each of the school sites. We invite a parent liaison from each school site to a meeting of our central parent group which gives them the sense of the larger parent network. I've had twenty parent meetings at school sites so far this year."

Cary was born in Merced, California. He spent his first four or five years abroad because his father was in the service. The family came back to the San Francisco Bay Area, and he grew up in San Francisco, receiving his pre-college schooling in the San Francisco School District. He went to a community college, then transferred to UC Berkeley where he received his undergraduate degree.

Who along the way exerted an influence? "My parents," he says. "Both my parents were college-educated. My mother was an elementary school teacher for 26 years, and my uncle was a physics professor at Cal Poly, San Luis Obispo. So I came from a well-educated family that valued education, which is not uncommon in the black community although a lot of people don't recognize that."

Cary has two children, six and nine. He is concerned about how they are being treated in school. "Teacher expectations of them are far lower than I know their abilities to be. Schools have assumptions about children, particularly children of color, particularly poor children of color. Expectations for them are low.

"In MESA we cast as wide a net as possible, knowing every child and every parent won't take advantage of it. Part of the reason, as I see it, is that the light has gone out and they don't see the possibilities. Some kids will get it and some won't. We just keep on truckin' with the ones who get it and we always keep the door open for the others."

Cary advocates expanding the program, not only to every school in the state but nationwide. One thing parents like about MESA: it provides prestige for their children being smart.

"It's okay to come to a place where you can really show your stuff and you're with other children of like mind," Cary says. "We are great role models in that sense, and we can visit any kind of school and set up a successful program. The model works in low-income schools and it will work in wealthy schools for underachieving rich kids. Why? Because we attend to the needs of children."

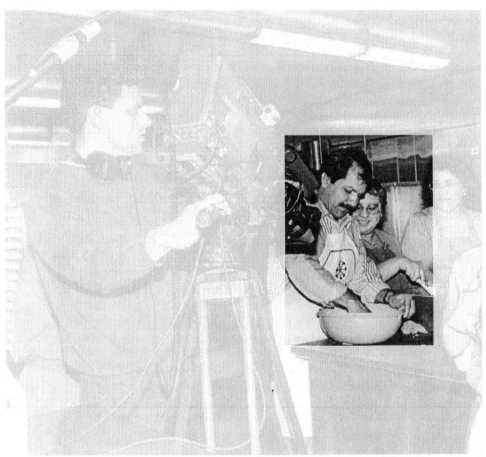

KTVU films MESA parents making tamales for afundraiser in Ukiah

Chapter 7
How the Program Works

One basic MESA program premise rests on the fact that communities fund public schools so children can acquire the academic fundamentals they need to be contributing citizens. This includes teaching college preparatory courses. MESA, therefore, designed activities that complement and augment, rather than duplicate, the efforts of educators. Much like knowledgeable and concerned parents, MESA will:

Supervise a student's study activities and academic course and college selection.

Support the student's interests with hands-on activities and work experiences while arranging opportunities for contacts with professionals in specific areas of interest.

Offer rewards for excellent performance and outstanding effort.

Study assistance: This fundamental MESA program service teaches students how to study and, especially, provides group study skills which allow them to succeed in these courses. Good study techniques abound. Many private concerns teach them for a fee, but MESA-targeted students rarely get an opportunity to learn these skills. The lack of study skills, so crucial for success in competitive, advanced mathematics and science courses, remains as one of the greatest barriers to MESA students' academic achievement.

The first priority of any high school MESA program is to raise the level of academic achievement of the student participants. Sessions that include the use of both individual and group study techniques achieve this goal.

The group study model, proposed at the first MESA Advisors Institute in 1978, was developed by Dr. Uri Treisman at the University of California,

Berkeley. Dr. Gerard Poirier, who supervised student teachers at UCB, presented an additional model for group activities in the classroom setting. During the 1980s, Poirier and Treisman presented workshops attended by MESA advisors, students, and parents. They emphasized the need for MESA high school students to learn how to use group study as a survival technique that would help them win their tough collegiate competition battles.

Each MESA center staff supports the school study programs in these varied ways:

1. Providing workshops in group study techniques for advisors, parents, and students.
2. Recruiting and hiring study resource persons who help each MESA school. Some are volunteers and include students enrolled in the MESA school.
3. Providing advisors funds to hire a few peer tutors who can be available to students on a more regular basis than the outside tutors.

The MESA program emphasizes group study because Treisman found that successful students enrolled in math-based university courses regularly used this technique, whether formal or informal. He also found this is a technique least used by African-American and Mexican-American students in predominantly white schools. One of MESA's influential contributions remains its method of helping students learn how to get the most academic value from their involvement with other students and contacts with their teachers.

Scholarship incentive awards: These demonstrate that the program places its highest emphasis on academic excellence. Students achieve eligibility with at least a semester completed and enrollment in mathematics, science, and English courses above the basic college requirements of geometry, biology, and second-year English. To receive this basic award, typically $100 at most centers, students must achieve a grade of B or better in each of three specified math, science, and English courses. Additionally, students must achieve a minimum PSAT or SAT score as determined by each center, using 900 as a base. Achieving test scores and grades above the minimum levels earns a student up to $200 each semester.

Scholarship awards to high school students were, from the outset, a vital part of the MESA program's success. Students from economically handicapped families often work, helping meet expenses. Cash awards for high academic achievement make studying the part-time job rather than working at a fast-food restaurant.

In the early days, some people argued that students should not be paid for grades, but should study for "the love of learning." MESA staff members pointed out that affluent families commonly gave their children cash and other rewards for academic achievement.

The financial incentive concept came of age in 1981 when self-made millionaire Eugene Lang offered to pay for the college education of sixty-one sixth grade students in Harlem's P.S. 121, his alma mater, if they completed high school. Fifty of them made it. Lang established the "I Have a Dream" program, which, he discovered, had to include program elements similar to MESA's.

Students who succeed because of good study habits also can learn the personal satisfaction of academic achievement. The MESA awards prove a more powerful tool for change than punishment or scolding. Awards capture the students' attention. Later, they strive for high standards because of the pride and satisfaction academic success gives them.

"During the first years of the program we discovered the awards played an important role, one we didn't anticipate," says Mary Perry Smith. "The quarterly checks, particularly for the males, gave a necessary male excuse for studying. In the tough neighborhoods, a good student was not recognized by his peers. Earning money, however, was."

A popular basketball court next to the home of Brandon Hewitt posed a challenge. He avoided the stigma of transporting homework by having a duplicate set of books at home so he could study in the attic. After the checks came, he showed his friends, bragging about how smart he was. Attitudes began changing.

He and other MESA graduates repeatedly thanked Smith and other advisors for the incentive awards. The money earned the respect of their peers and helped them survive in their communities while achieving A and B grades.

Hewitt was a MESA student at Oakland Tech for three years, earned a civil engineering degree at UC Berkeley and is now vice president of an engineering consulting firm in Birmingham.

"The program provided money if you made good grades in math, science, and English," he says. "I wanted that money, so I made sure I made those good grades."

Members of MESA center boards and staffs originated additional awards for ineligible students—those attending elementary or middle schools or in the first two years of high school academic work. MESA gives students at every grade level some type of recognition for academic achievement. Industry often sponsors special awards ranging from luncheons to gifts of hand calculators.

Academic Advising: This rates as the second most important service for students. The fabric of college requirements, as they relate to the names and content of high school courses, often befuddles even a school's own faculty and staff. Parents who follow their children's progress through high school sometimes receive incorrect information about the courses colleges require as prerequisites for specific majors. School counselors do not deliberately mishandle information. Instead, parents traditionally have guided their children through this information maze, using school counselors as just one of their resources.

Today, both MESA parents usually work and many families are headed by a single parent. This leaves little time for monitoring their children's course selections. Additionally, few MESA parents have completed college and some did not graduate from high school. Their inexperience and the hard-to-access information about college admission and course requirements particularly affect the careers of students interested in specialized fields. Even when counselors and parents go all out so students complete high school graduation and college admission requirements, the students may still find they met admission requirements but not the necessary prerequisites for college majors in engineering, mathematics, and science.

One reason MESA evolved was to assure that participants got the advice and support they needed to complete prerequisite courses. MESA advisors play the critical role in monitoring participants' course selection throughout high school. They must know the content and function of each math, science and English course in which MESA students enroll. Further, the advisors stay informed about the standards teachers of those courses require of their students. If these standards fall below what MESA accepts, the advisors move MESA students to a class with higher standards.

Some MESA advisors have turned around entire math and science departments in inner city and rural communities. In some cases, they boldly sought the aid of principals when teaching standards needed raising. Some students who attended a MESA summer program at USC told their advisor their chemistry instruction fell short at their inner city school. She encouraged the teacher to accept the assistance of a Cal Tech chemistry lecturer who volunteered to work with the teacher. The advisor found the teacher willing and eager.

"Public school teachers have learned to dread the opening quarter of the school year," Smith says. "Just as you get your classes organized, students working and involved, the district office begins shifting teachers from schools with low enrollment to those with unexpectedly high enrollments. The disruptions are often monumental because they affect the ability of students to complete courses they need or which interest them. Teachers sometimes lose entire classes and often have a shift of one-quarter to one-half of the students in their classes. A month or more of learning is lost each year in addition to the loss of learning during the two and a half months of summer."

One creative solution to a problem faced by a MESA advisor came during the early years of the program's expansion to a statewide level. Beleaguered counselors in a MESA school, trying to balance class enrollments after the district office had pulled teachers out of that school, decided to drop the classes in physics and pre-calculus mathematics. Dropping those classes meant that MESA students could not meet MESA graduation requirements. and the school faced the prospect of dropping from the program.

MESA advisors at PG&E Learning Center workshop —Photo by John Jernegan

"Please reinstate the classes," the MESA advisor pleaded. The principal, formerly a mathematics and science teacher, sympathized, but could not overrule his counselors in his first year in the post. He offered, however, to teach the students precalculus after school. The MESA advisor arranged for the class to meet at a nearby community college and, with a go-ahead from its president, lined up a college instructor for the physics class from 4:30 to 6:30 p.m. It proved a win-win situation for everyone involved.

MESA expects its high school graduates to compete in calculus, physics, chemistry, and English during their first year in college. As a result of good academic advising, MESA students do not need make-up courses.

MESA advisors also do academic advising in support of the work of the regular counseling staff. Overworked counselors do not have time and often lack the expertise needed to deal with the detailed advising students need in each career area. The most effective job of academic advising in a specific subject-matter major can be done by the teachers who themselves have majored in these areas. Some of the best academic advising in secondary schools is done by the business and coaching staffs for students with particular talents in these courses.

"It is about time for those who teach in other academic areas to similarly select and coach students with talents in fields such as mathematics, science, English, history, and humanities," says Smith. "The MESA model encompasses this concept."

Saturday Academies are a regular part of the enrichment activities of many Junior MESA programs. In the UC Berkeley MESA program, Victor Cary, center

—Photo by John Jernegan

UC Berkeley Saturday Academy staff—
(front left to right) Fred Easter, Laura
Darby, John Griego, (back left to right)
Chris Johnson, Victor Cary, Myra Grant.

director, found the key to attracting students he'd targeted for participation. He marketed the academy as an outstanding program with a limited, select enrollment and required that students apply for admission. He also opened the classes to MESA-targeted students enrolled in non-MESA schools and charged these families a fee for their youngsters' participation. A MESA Saturday Academy reinforces and expands upon what students learn in the school year. They build models and complete projects in hands-on activities that illustrate and deepen a student's understanding of math and science principles. Students working together in groups complete projects which they may enter in MESA Day competitions. Once students experience success with projects, some continue their work and later enter them in local science fairs. These experiences also make students more knowledgeable about their career options.

The middle school years often determine whether students, particularly boys, excel in their academic studies. They need to feel successful in their school work since they also experience difficult, confusing physical and social pressures. The academies stabilize and support middle school students, helping them stay focused on their school work. Succesful senior high MESA students serve as facilitators and mentors in Saturday academies around the state. They make excellent role models.

Parents at UC Berkeley often drove their children to sessions and waited for them. Then they decided to do more than just sit, talk and wait. First, they organized a parents club and helped monitor the halls and then provided lunch for the students. They saw their children having a great time and asked for some background information. Cary organized science and math activities for them. From this small beginning, led by MESA parent Laura Darby, the parents' activities now include classes in family math and science taught by parents trained at the Lawrence Hall of Science. University representatives conduct sessions that help parents understand college admission and financial aid requirements.

Saturday academies, effective vehicles for developing scholars, also help parents become partners with MESA in providing children with rich educational experiences.

Leadership Camps: Verna Benzler, former center director at Fresno State University, developed a one-week leadership camp for students around the state who serve as officers of their schools' MESA program. These include MESA Day and MESA club planning for each of the schools. Students receive training in leadership techniques and responsibilities and learn problem-solving methods. They evaluate the successful and the ineffectual activities and collaborate on improvements.

Contests: During the school year, students participate in other enrichment activities such as mathematics or science contests. These occur within a school, between MESA schools, or may involve MESA schools within a region. Non-MESA organizations often sponsor the regional math or science contests. Center directors and advisors enter their MESA students in these events, giving them opportunities to compete against the range of students they will likely meet in college. Larry Lim, USC Center director, sponsored the first Math Day for Southern California MESA students. Nearly all of the Southern California centers participate, helping several hundred youngsters develop and hone their math knowledge into competitive skills.

Summer programs: As MESA expanded, directors found more and more school districts unable to fund academic summer programs. MESA students need enrichment experiences because so many of them attend schools that lack the academic competition they will meet in college. From the first year, Professor Bill Somerton and Beth Cobb provided experiences that enriched and improved students' abilities.

Early on, emphasis was placed on helping students get summer jobs. The Steering Committee believed students needed the hands-on experience of working at meaningful tasks. Industry and university representatives reviewed techniques for getting the greatest mileage out of job interviews. Most MESA students had never worked. Once they started, they felt the sense of accomplishment from being paid for the work. They acquired the ability to write a resume and present a positive impression during an interview, how and when to ask questions about assignments, plus reporting on time and calling in when sick. These seem basic, but students without experience need orientation before tackling job assignments.

Students improved their leadership skills by preparing and presenting reports that evaluated the summer work experiences. Younger students, still a year away from similar situations, gained valuable information at these sessions. Some of the early MESA students worked in engineering and science related industries and offices where black and brown faces had never been seen as workers. These students had to deal not only with holding a first time job, but also with working in what were, to them, foreign, sometimes hostile environments.

At each company, a contact person who was also a MESA supporter, was identified for the students as a troubleshooter. MESA staff members prepared students for difficult situations that might arise, imbuing them with the concept that they represented the entire program and had a responsibility to perform well so future MESA students would be hired.

This MESA support system enhanced their work learning opportunities. Whether the students felt the job furnished a positive, neutral, or negative impact, the experiences almost always helped them mature. Their growing confidence after one or two summer jobs delighted MESA staffers, teachers, and parents.

Students too young for work enrolled in established summer programs at other institutions, some in other states. Several institutions received government funds and recruited youngsters nation-wide for two-week, hands-on pre-engineering residential programs. MESA helped students apply and they were highly recruited because they were so well prepared and focused on science and engineering.

In addition, some MESA students took advantage of summer programs operated by Upward Bound and the Professional Development Program. By carefully selecting summer experiences and using the large pool of government-funded programs many universities offered, MESA provided its students with a range of experiences without needing to raise money for its own summer schools. In 1975, MESA began developing its own summer enrichment programs, complementing the summer jobs and summer institutes some students enjoyed.

These first summer programs ran only two weeks. MESA staff members gave high school students challenging academic experiences, but not for credit. MESA does not duplicate the teaching curriculum public schools offer. It can include special topics that public schools lack the time for, and involve students in group study sessions, independent study and group projects. Public schools seldom can teach these college survival skills.

MESA's summer programs supplement and expand the regular school experience by including more hands-on work, individual study, problem solving and academic coping skills. Teachers discourage "school as usual"—students working from the same texts used during the school year. However, a few center directors, unhappy with the quality of instruction in some schools, have been known to spend part of the summer school day completing the books public school teachers only got half-way through.

Most summer programs take place on university campuses and involve students from all the schools serviced by the area's MESA center. Students work in the various science and engineering labs college students use. Both university faculty and secondary school teachers teach in these programs. College students often serve as assistants and tutors, and also as role models. MESA students learn to feel comfortable in a college setting. The core of each program includes enrichment in math, science and English appropriate for each grade level. Students do lab work, take field trips, hear speakers and participate in workshops that improve their study, interview and resume writing skills.

On the UC Berkeley campus, the summer program involves nearly all of the university-sponsored outreach programs that assist secondary schools. By pooling their resources, rather than duplicating efforts, the programs service a larger number of students and offer them a wider choice of academic experiences. Non-MESA families that can afford it enroll their children in these programs for a fee.

Some MESA centers conduct programs in the facilities of engineering corporations and have access to their computer training labs and technical equipment areas. During the late Seventies, the San Jose MESA Center held two three-week sessions at the Stanford Linear Accelerator. Students arose early and, after a bus ride each morning alongside San Francisco Bay, received physics lectures, including basic concepts of thermodynamics. Afterwards they gathered on the building's roof and built solar energy panels from scratch. They not only measured and sawed the wood for the panel frames, they also wrapped the copper wire for the coils that delivered the electricity the sun generated.

MESA Day: Bob Rice, a retired Berkeley High science teacher and the school's first MESA advisor, was known in the San Francisco-Oakland Bay Area as "Mr. Science Fair." While serving on MESA's Board of Directors, he worried about the paucity of underrepresented minority students entering projects in the Science Fair or its advanced level, the Junior Science and Humanities Symposium in which he was involved. Smith observed that MESA students lacked support systems young people need to develop and complete competitive projects. So Bob Finnell suggested organizing for students the equivalent of a MESA advisors' workshop. The activity was called MESA Day.

The first one came in April, 1982 on the UC Berkeley campus. Northern California MESA students were invited. During the morning they gathered for a science magic demonstration and lecture and in the afternoon they gathered in small groups according to their interests and grade levels. Each group made two site visits to campus labs in chemistry, physics or engineering and at the

Lawrence Berkeley Laboratory. During lunch, students watched as their oil derricks, built of toothpicks and glue, underwent strength tests. The team with the strongest derrick won prizes, providing it was built according to specific construction rules.

Two weeks later, MESA students in Southern California participated in their first MESA Day on the campus of Cal Tech. The host for the day: Lee Browne, a distinguished high school chemistry teacher, lecturer at Cal Tech and a MESA board member.

Current MESA Days include more hands-on activities and competitions, including an egg drop, math olympics and writing contests. Middle school youngsters take part in their own Junior MESA Day with events appropriate for their academic levels. MESA centers take turns hosting these activities, which require a major effort to organize since as many as 1,000 young people may attend. Many of their parents take part; they help run some activities and supervise students on buses.

Youngsters who first participate see themselves as part of a large network of students focused upon academic achievement in math and science. For some underrepresented minority students, this realization can determine whether or not they persist toward their career goals. Too often, they stand out as loners when they enroll in advanced mathematics and science classes, especially if they prove to be competitive with others. A support system for them, not only within the school but around the state, gives them a sense of security. Contacts made with students from other schools and districts at MESA Day often lead to lasting friendships based on a mutual goal of high academic achievement.

Parent meetings: "Successful schools take time to involve parents in their children's education," says Smith. "Even though students are under the supervision of schools seven hours a day, the parents must reinforce the educational process the rest of the time for students to succeed in difficult academic courses. For legal reasons, teachers must acquire parental/guardian approval for them to participate in evening or off-campus activities. MESA took this one step

Senior MESA Day at UC Irvine
—Photo by John Jernegan

further and sought the support of parents whose youngsters participated in the program."

The first orientation meeting with MESA parents took place during the fall of 1970. Their children invited them to a kickoff dinner that, because of limited funds, was mercifully prepared and served by members of the Oakland First Christian Church, which also hosted the event. MESA representatives welcomed both returning and new students, along with their parents, and gave them an overview of its purpose, requirements and projected activities. The founders and members of the Steering Committee attended and stayed for chats with the parents.

Impressed by the interest of university professors, the parents met the teachers and some of the tutors. Parents also shared ideas about how they could participate as members of the MESA team.

"This was a great beginning of parent involvement," says Smith.

From those original gatherings, MESA has urged parental participation. It rates as an important component of every pre-college MESA program. Some center directors organize parent groups that create their own bylaws, procedures, and fund raising activities, supplementing the work of paid staff.

Parents host study groups in their homes, supervise weekend activities, provide lunches for students in Saturday academies, speak as successful role models, tutor, raise funds, and serve as MESA advocates at school board and community meetings. Data from MESA centers confirms that programs with the best results have the most effective parental involvement.

Year-end banquets: MESA program activities slow down when high school seniors begin the hectic graduation countdown. Anything MESA might schedule easily could submerge in the frenzy. The challenge of honoring those qualifying participants became part of the planning process even during the first year.

Somerton, along with Somerville and Cobb, felt strongly that MESA representatives should encourage the seniors who graduated the first year. A luncheon was arranged in June, 1970. "Let's ask all of the seniors to talk about their career plans," the founders decided. "They can tell how MESA influenced their choice of the college or university they're attending." This made seniors the focus of the lunch and set the tone for future banquets. The first one consisted of sandwiches, soft drinks and dessert served on eight-foot-long tables in an Oakland Tech classroom. The founders communicated their hopes for the group with a simple, "You have done good work in high school. Now we expect to see you get the job done in college."

The seniors' comments inspired not only their peers but the adults as well. Somerville instilled in these early MESA students that it was **their** program and welcomed their ideas. Their representatives attended meetings of the Advisory Board. "That day, there was little doubt in anyone's mind that MESA would work," says Smith. "The seniors, with only one semester in MESA, had absorbed its essence. They spoke frankly to the juniors and sophomores about the need for hard work to meet MESA standards."

Over the years this annual "MESA family" gathering developed into one of its most important program components. It sends graduates to the next educational level knowing the pride people feel about them and their achievements. The attention and honors renew and reinforce their commitments toward achieving personal and professional goals. They embark knowing they serve as role models whose success can encourage others.

In some centers, banquets attract more than five hundred students and family members as well as industry, university, school district, public official, and community representatives. Banquets take place in school and industry cafeterias, hotels, and convention centers.

In 1982, Verna Benzler, Fresno MESA Center director, took to heart the training she received on making the year-end banquet an effective public relations tool. She invited then Governor Jerry Brown to be her keynote speaker. After all, he was running for reelection and she was offering an audience of up to 250 people representing an ethnic and economic cross-section of voters.

Nearly daily conversations with the governor's campaign staff got continuing commitments that he would show. As the day and then the hour approached, his staff began waffling. Benzler stood firm, knowing she would face, for years, the disappointed students and teachers and the "I told you so's." She stayed on the phone as he made whistle-stop appearances across the state. Finally, holding her audience past 11 p.m. after the awards and other speeches had ended, she received word the governor's plane had landed. Suffice it to say, he received one of the biggest ovations of his campaign. The warm response didn't stem the tide, however. He lost the election in November.

The annual banquet is the ribbon that ties MESA program elements together. It can renew one's faith in future generations, as the husband-and-wife team of Evelyn and Domingo Torres-Rangel can attest. These teachers at Woodrow Wilson High School in East Los Angeles attended the 1992 banquet that marked the end of their seven-year stint as MESA co-advisors. Near the end of the affair, MESA students took control, to the surprise of the organizers. They presented the couple with an engraved plate with the inscription, "Thank you for all your love and support." Domingo says, "They put 'love' first and 'support' second. I couldn't hold back my tears. Then when we were going out of the room, people stood up and clapped. I've never before had people stand up and clap for me. It was pretty overwhelming."

Zelma Allen:
Holding Students
Responsible for Excellence

It was a case of the right person at the right time in the right place.

High schools in the southwest section of Los Angeles offered only the courses required for graduation in the early 1980s.

"They didn't provide the academic courses students needed for college admission in math-related fields," says Zelma Allen. "Their counselors didn't seem to know how to steer kids into engineering. Courses billed as computer science, for example, were, in fact, business data processing courses."

With characteristic understatement she adds, "We were able to fix a lot of that."

The fix came after Allen, a City of Los Angeles employee, got hooked on MESA, but it would take seven years to reel her in.

"I was in the engineering department, which became the first group outside a university to sponsor a MESA program," she says. "I took a leave of absence to serve as MESA's director at Southwest Community College."

Like many colleges of its type, Southwest offered mostly courses for general education, self-help and vocations. Help came from MESA centers at UCLA and CSU Northridge, even though MESA then regarded community colleges as dead ends for students interested in engineering and science.

"We realize now that a community college can serve as a great resource for students, but only if there's a person on the campus who knows what they need," she says.

Southwest Community College is a hub for half a dozen high schools. Allen began by persuading school district superintendent George McKenna, who was then vice principal at Washington High, to teach a trigonometry class, after first convincing the Southwest administrators that thirty high schoolers would hardly be noticed on campus from 4 to 7 p.m.

"It worked well," says Allen, a Dallas, Texas native who began college at the age of sixteen in pre-med., then switched to business information systems and math. "Oh, some of the instructors who didn't live in the neighborhood had a negative view of what the students could do. Some people assumed there was no future

Zelma Allen

for all those children. They never paid attention to the fact that a big percentage of them went to college."

She successfully persuaded Southwest to provide algebra 1 and 2 courses consecutively, instead of interrupting them with a year of geometry.

"Geometry makes no sense to students in the eighth, ninth or tenth grade. It requires deductive reasoning and they haven't developed that faculty at that age. The high schools were embarrassed. They gave A's and B's to students who memorized, but didn't understand, theorems, then didn't do well at all on their SATs. Students who got C's in geometry at Southwest scored over 1,000 on their SATs because they could reason better."

In 1988, Southwest paid her the compliment of asking her to include some community college students in the MESA program. It was about this time she decided to resign from the City of Los Angeles, making the MESA tie official, even though it meant a smaller salary package.

She estimates that only about one out of ten community colleges provides the monitoring, counseling, and courses needed for students interested in transferring to four-year colleges and universities.

"When I was growing up in Texas, teachers would embarrass or reprimand us. You could get your hand spanked. And you learned how to behave. Well, those things are obsolete now, but we do make the students do the work by holding them responsible for excellence. We let them know we won't accept mediocrity. They know we care about them."

Allen also involves parents with two meetings per year and numerous individual contacts. She's doing it now at Loyola Marymount University in Los Angeles. She became MESA center director there in 1989. The challenges range from undocumented, sometimes illiterate Mexican students to the loss of MESA high school advisors who, buffeted by pay cuts and crowded classes, go elsewhere to teach. To cope, she continues the strategy that worked before: holding students responsible for excellence.

Laura Darby
Taps a Resource

Laura Darby plays a dual role in her MESA involvement. She works full time at the UC Berkeley Engineering Dean's office as coordinator of parental involvement for several programs, including MESA and MESA Minority Engineering Programs. Her daughter, Kristin, also is a MESA student. Earlier, Laura Darby was an employee with the MESA Statewide Office so she was well aware of the program. She first got involved in the parental support program after her daughter joined the Saturday Academy program as an independent student from a non-

MESA targeted school. The program ran from 9 a.m. to 1 p.m.

"Many parents brought their children and just sat around for several hours," she says. "Some of them gathered and decided they would prepare a light lunch for the children after they completed their classes. This brought the

Laura Darby

parents together and they would sit around and talk about various things. Word got around and more and more parents would come and they realized that they were forming a group."

At this point, Darby visited Victor Cary, director of the UC Berkeley MESA Center. "Victor, it seems to me we ought to be able to at least get these people together and just talk to them in an organized fashion; give them some information. Maybe we should have someone come and talk to us about the program, college entrance requirements, and other topics of interest to parents. You've got these people sitting there for several hours. Let's do something."

"Okay, if you think you can organize it and get the parents together, go ahead," he replied.

That's how the workshops began. Persons with expertise in various fields, including some of the parents, talked to the group.

MESA centers, Darby knew, always need volunteer help and who could better do this than parents of MESA students, she mused.

"I decided to hold an organizing meeting and bring all this energy together," said Darby. "I soon realized there were a lot of resources within the parent group and I just had to know how to corral this. We set up committees responsible for specific activities. We organized an awards banquet committee, taking the load of this activity off the shoulders of the MESA staff. We organized a fund-raising committee, a parents' newsletter committee and committees for parent outreach and parent field trips. We formed a steering committee and as more and more parents became involved, we appointed co-chairs for each committee."

To assist other groups in setting up a parent support program, an original group member developed a generic charter adaptable to various situations. Darby, in her role as an employee of the dean's office, now uses this charter when she helps set up parent support groups for local school MESA programs.

"My daughter, Kristin, was in the fifth grade at a non-MESA targeted parochial school," Darby says. "Knowing the benefits of the program, I prevailed upon the assistant director of the Saturday Academy to let her attend. He agreed and Kristin, who is now in the ninth grade, has been in the Saturday program ever since and has attended three summer programs. The first summer she was ready to divorce me and my mother was going to disinherit me because she thought I was being totally cruel to make Kristin attend class five days a week all day and still do homework at night. Summer was not for that. Now she's doing wonderfully well. She's on the honor roll and made the dean's list. I attribute a lot of what Kristin has accomplished to the MESA program. It's not just the academic preparation, but the motivational environment as well plays an important role. She's learned the lesson that, 'I can do it,' the self confidence, the knowing, 'I belong there and I'm willing to work for it,' all from this program. She really loves those field trips. They expose her to a lot of different things, things I wouldn't have been able to do for her independently. I can't say enough about the program because I really believe that it works. It's definitely had a very positive influence in my daughter's life."

Evelyn and Domingo Torres-Rangel: A Knack for Nurturing

To raise money for MESA activities and field trips, Evelyn and Domingo Torres-Rangel drove groups of their Woodrow Wilson High School students to TV game and quiz shows.

"They told us if we brought forty students we'd get a bonus prize, so we showed up with forty-one," says Domingo Torres-Rangel. 'You have your choice of one of three prizes,' they said. One was a pair of sunglasses, the other was a queen size mattress and the third prize was by a mail order company where you order steaks by mail. I said, 'Okay. I'll take the steaks.'"

Soon afterward eighty filet mignon steaks, marinated, went onto the barbecues in the Torres-Rangel's back yard.

Evelyn and Domingo Torres-Rangel (center, standing) with students

"We invited all the MESA kids over and it was a lot of fun," says Domingo. He and his wife served as MESA advisors from 1985 at the East Los Angeles school where 93 percent of the students are of Mexican-American descent. In that first year, Woodrow Wilson High offered one class in chemistry. In 1992, thanks to MESA's influence, five chemistry classes existed.

The two MESA advisors had their students in the program form a cabinet made up of elected officers. That didn't quite work so the defeated candidates were invited. As a result, a good mix of ideas surfaces at their meetings. "We call it the Advisory Committee," says Evelyn. "It works out a lot better than just a small core group.

"At the beginning of the year, we see students who are shy, you can barely hear them speak. I encourage them to stand up and say something, and by the end of the year, they're outspoken and aggressive."

Leon Mendoza, as twelfth-grade MESA president, came up with an idea of asking experienced MESA students to adopt tenth graders, much like Big Brothers/Big Sisters, answering questions and providing encouragement. Raphael Viegas, a candidate, it seemed, for a neighborhood gang, became a MESA leader instead. It was Raphael who persuaded cabinet members that the group's minimum qualifying grade level should rise from C to C+, saying, "If I can do it, all of you can too."

Evelyn still remembers the day when their team, which was expected to take the third place prize, won the MESA Day Math Olympics. "A team consists of three members and they take the same test, but work individually," she says. "Their combined score is tallied versus the combined scores of the other teams. We work with them sometimes, but we encourage them to study to-gether. You know, a lot of times we glorify athletics, which is great, but this gives a chance for the academic kids to receive recognition."

Ina Roth, Woodrow Wilson High assistant principal, says MESA doesn't give students false hopes. "Some of them aspire to be movie stars and, unprepared for failure, they may drop out. MESA tells them, 'Okay, you didn't achieve that goal, now try this.' MESA focuses them on something. When they have direction, they're more likely to stay in school."

Evelyn's influence was summed up by Antonio Gonzalez who recalls, "I was a questionable student, not too interested in my education. My appearance was not impressive because I had dyed my hair. But Ms. T.R. treated me like any other student and gave me her full attention when I needed her."

In a letter nominating her for the Teacher of the Year Award, he cites the open door policy at both her classroom and home, her willingness to help with personal problems, and the activities outside school in which she participates. "Ms. T.R. has taught me moral values; among these is being unselfish because she sets the most perfect example," he states. "I hope to someday be an influential person to one needy student just like Ms. T.R. influenced me."

Evelyn and Domingo, winners of the Mary Perry Smith Award for outstanding work as advisors, were featured in the Los Angeles Times after they began teaching on alternate years, so one of them would be at home with their two young sons.

"Your kids learn 50 percent of what they learn from the ages of zero to five," he told the reporter. "We wanted to have as much influence on them as possible."

The alternating posed financial hardships, some misunderstandings for him and his discovery that it's harder being at home than working.

Julian Zaragoza:
Part of the MESA Family

"In a conversation about recarpeting the office, Julian Zaragoza can tell you whether it's useful programmatically or not, and once he has decided that, as far as he's concerned that's the end of the discussion. I like working with someone like that. It's easy to lose sight of the kids when you're performing these administrative functions."

The speaker, Fred Easter, executive director of MESA Statewide, says his director of programs has an unerring knack for finding the programmatic issue. Zaragoza fills the position originally held by Mary Perry Smith. In any extended discussion, he invariably brings up her name for he tries to emulate her principles.

"MESA succeeds because of its simplicity," he declares, then quotes her, saying, "Keep that focus on MESA because that's the reason for its success."

He attributes his own success to Smith's training.

Before coming to MESA Zaragoza worked as a probation/child treatment counselor for Los Angeles County. His relations with McClaren Hall's neglected, abandoned and abused children left him concerned about the small number of children he could help. When an opening for a half-time MESA coordinator at California State University, Long Beach, occurred in 1978, he jumped at the chance of serving more children in a proven, constructive manner. The position soon became full time, and he served at CSU Long Beach six years before joining the Statewide staff in Berkeley.

Today, he spends about two-thirds of his time in the field visiting with the twenty MESA pre-college centers. He works with center directors, school advisors and MESA students, trouble-shooting, encouraging, inspiring, supporting, and cajoling. He is their teacher, their champion, their critic, and their friend. The 1992 budget crunch aroused his concern.

"Directors scurry to obtain new funding sources so the program can grow but, in so doing, they become involved in other things than taking care of the shop. Thank God for the teachers who serve as school-site advisors; they run the program. However, the advisors suffer from the lack of training and support from the center directors."

One of Zaragoza's biggest responsibilities is making arrangements for an annual MESA Advisors Training Institute. From 1987 through 1992 it was held at Pacific Gas & Electric Company's Learning Center in San Ramon, California. As many as 250 MESA school-site advisors attend this weekend program of training sessions, workshops, discussion groups, banquets, and award ceremonies. PG&E handled most of the tab for lodging and meals while other industrial sponsors paid for travel expense and awards. Professionals, most of whom volunteer their services, lead the workshops.

"Teachers who attend are recognized in a way they've never been recognized before, both in terms of the caliber of the workshops and their treatment as professionals."

There are comments from the participants

Julian Zaragoza

—Photo by John Jernegan

such as, "I don't know how you guys do it." "You get better and better every year." "This is the way school districts should do their in-service training." "I've never been as appreciated or felt as good as I do here."

The director of programs hits some roadblocks. Zaragoza recalls a high school in South San Francisco.

"The principal was having problems with the program because of the pressures and the things we were asking for. He said, 'Why? Black males are going to be in jail or they're on drugs, and black females are going to get pregnant. Mexican kids are going to be the gardeners and maids, so why in hell support the program?'"

Zaragoza has encountered attitudes like this before. He was born in Texas but grew up in East Los Angeles.

"I have sixteen half-brothers and half-sisters from four different women and my father, but I was raised by my grandmother. I remember my grandmother making T-shirts and boxer shorts out of flour sacks, not the 'in' thing like flour-sack shirts of today. I was a farm worker, picked oranges, apples and grapes. You name it, I've done it.

"I always knew education was the way out. I wasn't going to be a junkie, I was going to be a lawyer, a doctor, an aeronautical engineer. But when I went into that high school algebra class the teacher said, 'What the hell are you doing here? Your kind doesn't belong here. You sit at the back of the room and when I tell you, you open and close the door.'

"So I said, 'The hell with you,' and I dropped out of school. At the time, the Vietnam war was going on and I joined the Marine Corps. There was discrimination even there. I survived Vietnam and returned to work full time but went to school at night and completed my education."

In his fourteen years with MESA, Zaragoza has become one of its strongest advocates.

"The most impressive thing about it is what people think about it, feel about it, and do about it. The students, the teachers, the principals, the industry people really believe in it. They look at its successes. They have ownership of it; they expect excellence. They feel whoever it is in the MESA family—and MESA is a family—they can go to them and get the answer. They can get results.

"Like students at MESA Day saying, 'Yeah, it was hard. I didn't believe you, but it was hard, and I'm sure glad I did it.' That is the important thing about MESA. Students really think it's great. And it is. They hear other students say, 'You're a MESA student? Wow!' With MESA, you're going to be successful. You did it. You belong to the MESA family. It's throughout the organization from top to bottom, whether it's a paid professional, a volunteer, or whoever. They really believe in the program."

Chapter 8
Industry Involvement with MESA

From the earliest planning sessions, MESA program founders recognized the importance of linking with industry and business. Role model engineers who could meet with students on field trips and financial support from industry were both essential for program success. The earliest MESA committees included representatives from both public and private organizations employing engineers and scientists. Five years' experience with a few companies in the East Bay and San Francisco demonstrated the feasibility of industry participation in a secondary school activity by the time of MESA's expansion planning in 1977.

Nevertheless, in the mid-1970s corporate support and participation in secondary education proved the exception not the rule. Indeed, some people argued for limited participation or even rejected it. Throughout the post-World War II expansion of education, industry, and, for that matter, most foundations, concentrated their giving to postsecondary institutions. Engineering and scientific intensive industries often supported universities that provided them with graduates or where their key officers or board members graduated. Some companies encouraged their employees to become active in community activities, but their participation was often tied to their family needs and loyalties. Few participated actively as company policy or plan.

On the surface, the reasons are clear. Most viewed elementary and secondary school education as a local function tax resources supported. Since businesses were already taxed as local corporate citizens, they felt they'd already given their share. In addition, many companies wanted payoffs for their grants. And participation in secondary school education would make it difficult for them to tie their giving to the hiring of a particular employee ten years down the line. As an executive once said, "Our chairman likes to give a company grant to an engineering student when he or she completes their junior year, then hire that graduate a year later when he or she receives a B.S. degree." Obstacles like these loomed in the early and mid-1970s. Founders of MESA, a concept that itself bucked traditional approaches to minority education, recognized that unless they surmounted this hurdle, they faced difficult times expanding in one of the most scientific and engineering oriented states in America.

The original team developed a multi-faceted plan for industry involvement. Within five years its execution and success became the foundation for MESA's long term program as well as its expansion into other states and at other educational levels. The plan included:

1. Involving industry leaders on state and local MESA boards, both governing and advisory.
2. Expanding the number of companies participating.
3. Developing with companies a multi-leveled participation in the delivery of services to students.
4. Using the industry participation in MESA as a leverage with other institutions, public and private, for their support.

These key steps toward industry participation in MESA came during 1978 and 1979 as local MESA centers grew at a dozen sites around California. While these sites included some local industry support, the MESA Statewide Office at the Lawrence Hall of Science assumed the major responsibility for links with industry. The major linkage evolved by creating a MESA Industry Advisory Board. Participating companies each sent a representative and appointed a liaison for discussing the appropriate level of support each company provided to MESA.

Preliminary organization steps began after an exchange of letters between Dr. Roger Heyns, president of the Hewlett Foundation, and Stephen Bechtel, Jr., chairman of the board of the Bechtel Corporation. Bechtel agreed to encourage industry support for MESA and Richard Collins, a Bechtel vice president, was appointed as the initial chair of the Industry Advisory Board. He was assisted by Bruce Thiel, who served as MESA industry coordinator.

Letters to major California companies interested eleven additional companies. They endorsed participation and assigned high-ranking executives to serve on MESA's Industry Advisory Board and an additional person to serve as industry coordinator. The companies, endorsing chief executives and members included the following:

ARCO, Thorton Bradshaw, president; Lodwrick Cook, senior vice president; Chevron, H. J. Haynes, chairman; Tom Tupper, vice president;

MESA students at Chevron's computer center

Fluor Corporation, J. R. Fluor, chairman; Thomas Murphy, general manager;
Hewlett Packard Company, David Packard, chairman; Ken Capen, equal
    opportunity manager;
Lockheed Corporation, Roy A. Anderson, chairman; Tom Raleigh, senior
    vice president;
Northrop Corporation, Thomas V. Jones, chairman; Donald Warner, corpo-
    rate vice president;
Pacific Gas & Electric Company, Fred W. Mielke, chairman; Richard K.
    Miller, vice president;
Pacific Telephone, Gordon Hough, chairman; John Ball, assistant vice
    president;
Rockwell International Corporation, W. F. Rockwell, Jr., chairman; Patrick
    Crotty, staff vice president;
Southern California Edison Company, Jack Horton, chairman; David Fogarty,
    senior vice president;
TRW, Inc., Ruben E. Mettler, chairman; Dr. Robert Bromberg, vice presi-
    dent.

The appointment of the Industry Advisory Board fueled the key vehicle for
mobilizing corporate support for MESA. The first meeting took place on October

24, 1978, at the Lawrence Hall of Science. Subsequent meetings two or three times a year in various California cities gave board members chances to interact with local program representatives and gave them insights into the program operations. The Industry Advisory Board chairman also served on the MESA Board of Directors. Chairs of this board over the years are listed in Appendix II. From time to time one or more other corporate representatives joined him on MESA's governing board. The objectives of the MESA Industry Advisory Board included:

1. Coordinate financial and volunteer support from industry.
2. Communicate industry's role to universities, school boards, and professional groups.
3. Provide feedback to MESA program operations and evaluate program effectiveness.

Staff members used the initial meetings of the MESA Industry Advisory Board to explain in detail the goals, objectives, operations, plans, and results of the MESA secondary school program. In addition, sessions with each company's industry coordinator pinpointed specific actions it could carry out to support the program. Different companies handled their responses in different ways, usually depending on the relationship with local MESA centers. Several examples illustrate how corporate volunteer support with MESA Centers evolved:

Pacific Telephone's multiple locations in California allowed its representative, Gene Tatmon, to link each MESA center with a local PacTel liaison. After a series of meetings with MESA staff and visits to MESA centers around California, he developed a plan. It enabled local center directors to call nearby offices for field trips and speakers, place some students in summer employment, and in other ways enlist volunteer or in-kind contributions. He produced a handbook for company employees that ensured continuity for their support and management of the program from his office. In addition, several local center boards included Pacific Telephone representatives. A number of companies with statewide offices used this approach and model.

Hewlett-Packard took another approach when Harry Portwood identified more than fifteen employees who visited Berkeley for a briefing on the MESA program before the company's interface with MESA centers. Later, two of these employees played key roles in starting a MESA satellite center in Santa Rosa.

Other company industry coordinators dealt directly with local centers and arranged field trips, speakers, or provided other services, depending on their capabilities. MESA's expansion prompted unanticipated innovations that helped motivate students and communicated the companies' interest in their academic success. For example, AT&T's Long Lines office in San Francisco held an annual luncheon, recognizing juniors who achieved outstanding results. Dick Bowman, an AT&T manager, recognized that graduating seniors would get attention but worried about recognizing MESA students at some earlier point. Other companies began donating products, such as calculators, as awards for students who showed the most improvement in their school. As the years pro-

Students at PG&E's Diablo Canyon marine biology lab   —Photo by David Ball

gressed, the information shared by both original and new board members sparked ideas for activities or recognition awards for MESA students.

From the local center's point of view, the organizational work by the MESA Statewide Office brought broadscale services from industry, saving each director the detailed process of identifying, contacting, and requesting from company representatives field trips, speakers, and other services. Instead, company industry coordinators often called them. When center directors called, their requests were heard by informed, cooperative ears.

The companies' in-kind contributions initially did not appear on annual MESA budgets, but eventually records accumulated and estimates were made of corporate support. A mid-1980s study confirmed MESA's programs received approximately $1 million in volunteer time and related donations in one year. A decade earlier at the winter meeting of the National Advisory Council on Minority Employment, Inc., in Washington, D.C., Steve Bechtel, Jr., told the group, in explaining his support for MESA, "What we're after is a coordinated effort both to maximize the effectiveness of our financial and in-kind support and to ensure full integration of industry, university, local community, professional society, and state government resources." The Industry Advisory Board proved instrumental for MESA's use of corporate financial and in-kind support in a cooperative manner.

California industry and businesses fueled MESA with a level of student support and service beyond that envisioned in its original five-year plan. About the time the MESA Industry Advisory Board formed, the Hewlett Foundation awarded MESA a challenge grant of $100,000 contingent on raising an equal amount from industry. At that time MESA totally depended on its foundation funding. In seeking support, it emphasized the successful new center sites around the state, made a convincing case for cost-effectiveness, and mentioned the wastefulness of starting similar but parallel programs. As a result, California industry gave $105,000 in matching funds. Their generosity produced an additional impact.

In Sacramento legislative committees with educational responsibilities were searching for effective ways of increasing postsecondary opportunities for minority students. Sensing an opportunity, the MESA Board of Directors met in Sacramento for the first time and encouraged state officials to consider the MESA program as an option. Staff work followed and eventually produced a decision by the State of California to invest $250,000 in MESA. A crucial argument for this support was the active role played by industry and its own investments in MESA. Through the leveraging of private corporate and state funds, by 1979 MESA began matching its foundation support, thereby enhancing the possibility of serving students far beyond the five years envisioned by the initial foundation grants from Hewlett and Sloan.

By 1982 the hesitancy to invest in secondary school programs no longer prevailed. In a speech at the National Academy of Sciences on May 12, 1982, Edwin L. Harper, assistant for policy development to President Reagan, noted, "In California a group of major companies, in cooperation with local foundations and the state government,

Lockheed display at Southern California MESA Day

—Photo by John Jernegan

provides more than a million dollars a year to MESA, a program to help minority students prepare for technical careers."

By that time, MESA had already launched its "Project 920," a drive to raise $920,000 by July 1, 1983, so it could leverage a matching grant of $1,300,000 appropriated by the state legislature. Led by then Industry Advisory Board Chairman Lodwrick Cook of ARCO, the project also had a goal of increasing the corporate support base throughout California and informing a wider audience of the minority engineering crisis. Dennis Laurie, ARCO director of Corporate Community Relations, became the key advocate and leader in this project and thereby assured its success. ARCO paid the project expenses, produced a slide show, "The MESA Story," and arranged presentations around the state sponsored by leading corporations based in San Francisco, Los Angeles, Orange County, San Diego, and other cities. The state was divided into five regions and some three hundred companies were contacted during the campaign. Potential supporters learned about MESA at breakfast meetings. Students and advisors themselves attended these meetings, and their personal contact demonstrated the program's effectiveness.

At the June 30, 1983, board meeting Lod Cook revealed the results: seventy-five companies had contributed $1,100,000. This not only exceeded MESA's previous corporate level of $400,000 but also broadened the corporate base. In addition to more manufacturing and technology companies, names of banks, insurance companies, and accounting firms appeared on MESA's roster. As corporate funds leveraged the state funds, MESA seemed sure of maintaining its level of services to a large number of students beyond the initial five-year foundation grant period. Indeed, this campaign, by saturating the corporate community with the MESA message and successfully recruiting many of them to support the effort, ensured the organization's long-term viability. From the perspective of the 1990's, institutional support clearly was solidified by the Project 920 campaign.

A listing of companies providing financial support of $5,000 or more appears in Appendix III. Many other companies have provided smaller grants to MESA. Many foundations and public agencies have also provided financial support for MESA and are listed in Appendices IV and V.

As a consequence of the success of Project 920, industry involvement in MESA reached a sustaining plateau. The increased level and broad base of support also produced increased in-kind support to MESA students. Since financial resources couldn't buy the field trips, speakers, summer employment opportunities, and other in-kind corporate contributions, Project 920 also provided the increasing number of MESA students direct contact with scientific and engineering work, motivating their academic achievement and fostering their self-esteem; they recognized they were both needed and wanted in the mainstream of life in their community. This also stimulated the teachers and parents working in MESA by giving them the feeling of participating in a shared endeavor.

Most of the local corporate representatives to MESA centers attended end-of-the-year MESA recognition events and saw the parents, teachers, and students. While not as rigorous as educators' formal evaluations of MESA's effectiveness, the contacts made at these events placed human faces and voices instead of numbers and words in the minds of the corporate representatives. They could report back, "MESA is a worthwhile investment for our company."

The close interaction between corporate representatives and MESA eventually produced a major new line of support to MESA that began in 1982: companies began loaning personnel for one- or two-year periods at either the MESA Statewide Office or a local MESA center.

GE, Exxon, IBM, Bethlehem Steel, and others had loaned personnel to national and local organizations aiding minorities in the engineering field. Through the National Action Council for Minorities in Engineering, more than one hundred companies knew of secondary schools and universities serving minority students and preparing them for academic study in science and engineering fields. The NACME network, aware of MESA's expansion in California, also had an overview of efforts throughout the United States. As MESA expanded, it gave companies with executive loan programs a potential home for employees interested in working in the educational arena with minority students.

IBM sent one of its executives, Gene Houston, to work at MESA's Statewide Office. He arrived at a crucial time in 1982 when the MESA secondary school program was being expanded to serve university students. Using a model developed at CSU Northridge by Dr. Raymond Landis, Houston was assigned the task of translating the university level expansion proposal into an operational part of MESA. Working closely with the MESA centers, engineering schools, NACME's West Coast representative, Mike Macias (who had assisted MESA in developing the university level proposal), and others, Houston visited campuses, established a proposal process, and opened the university level centers across California. Later, he worked with Landis to set up training sessions for the MESA Minority Engineering Program directors.

Houston's successful stint with MESA led to a series of IBM loaned executives at the MESA Statewide Office and MESA centers in California. He was followed by Mel Bell, Lloyd Conaway, Mary Ann Carr, Nom Du and others over the next six years. Their skills strengthened MESA's long-range planning, development and training.

IBM's contribution in personnel to MESA has been substantial. The initial loaned executives recommended working also with local MESA centers and in subsequent years some IBM executives worked with local program directors.

The loaned executive program at MESA achieved another dimension in 1985 when Pacific Gas & Electric Company loaned Tim Kelly to MESA, where he worked for two years. He played a key role in sustaining and increasing corporate involvement in MESA activities, took part in the management and decision-making processes, and carried back to his company the value of the MESA program.

In 1988, PG&E began sponsoring an annual conference, which later became the MESA Advisor Training Institute. The early August meetings for teachers from MESA schools, hosted annually through 1992 at the San Ramon PG&E Training Center, featured outstanding speakers and discussion leaders who worked with MESA's secondary school team. The institutes boosted the morale of the teachers working with MESA, prepared them for their diverse duties in its program, and made an indelible impression.

In addition to the suport of Stephen Bechtel, Jr., and Richard Collins, other Bechtel personel have contributed in major ways in expanding the MESA concept. An example is Charles O'Neil, a project engineer for Bechtel, who helped establish the Arizona MESA project and has been a strong advocate for the program.

Studies at the peak of industry involvement indicated investments of more than $1 million annually by volunteer efforts associated with MESA. This includes the volunteer time of company representatives, the equipment and supplies they donated, and the cost of other services provided to MESA students or the program.

But the real measure and contribution is non-economic. At the high school level, for example, MESA measures its results by counting the number of graduates prepared to pursue a math-based field of study at the university level. At the university level it counts the number of MESA students who receive their engineering degrees. The role of industry in this realm also has significant non-economic value which is not as easily calculated by conventional accounting methods. For example, the week-to-week visibility of volunteers from key companies or engineering professions communicates a subtle but forceful message that MESA's minority students are wanted and valued. By taking time to tutor, host a field trip, act as a mentor, or speak to students, industry volunteers place a human face and figure on what was a distant or unknown profession or industry.

When MESA students hear a recent graduate in engineering speak and discover that, seven or eight years before, the visitor had been a MESA student, the students often conclude, "If he can do it, so can I." When they hear a company's top-level executive tell them they are needed to make that company innovative and efficient, this counters peer pressures that academic study doesn't count. This alternative, which can't be measured in conventional means, is an essential part of MESA. So while some may argue about the dollars-and-cents value of industry support, the MESA view has been to measure the results and recognize that the industry role is vital to producing that result.

Stephen D. Bechtel, Jr.:
Filling the Pipeline

Some MESA students admit, "I didn't even know what an engineer did." That wasn't the case for Steve Bechtel, Jr. He grew up in a family that was fashioning one of the top engineering and construction companies in the world and spent time at job sites such as Hoover Dam. He began working as a field engineer in 1948. Now he's chairman emeritus of Bechtel Group, Inc.

Despite a busy schedule running one of the nation's top engineering and construction firms, Bechtel found time to become an early supporter of MESA.

It began in 1977 with a call from Roger Heyns, then president of the Hewlett Foundation and a former chancellor of the University of California, Berkeley.

"He asked if I would provide the leadership in forming a consortium of San Francisco Bay Area companies that would assist in motivating and preparing high school minority students for college enrollment in engineering and the sciences," he recalls.

"I agreed to take on that effort and immediately contacted the CEOs of twelve major Bay Area companies. Shortly thereafter, MESA's Industry Advisory Committee was formed."

The Bechtel organization's involvement in the minority engineering effort actually had begun in 1973 when he became a charter member of the National Action Council for Minorities in Engineering under the auspices of the National Academy of Engineering. In 1981, the association became the "Action Council," better known as NACME. Bechtel helped guide the group's coordinated national effort, an experience he recalls as "very rewarding."

Bringing minority students into engineering college programs is only half

Steven D. Bechtel, Jr.

the battle, he said at a NACME conference.

"Once there, they also need the right kind of help to stay on course," he said. "We need to work with potential engineering students before they ever get to college, to ensure that they are ready in all respects for the tough grind ahead. They need better pre-college programs in mathematics, science, and English while still in high school to give them the basic tools they need. I think one of the finest programs in this respect is the MESA effort. It serves as a viable program that keeps filling the pipeline."

He is encouraged by industry's efforts in minority recruitment and by the influence companies exert to guide available funding toward effective programs such as MESA.

During nearly forty-five years with the organization, Bechtel has worked in assignments ranging from his 1948 starting job as field engineer to the head of a company known for developing some of the world's most complex, first-of-a-kind projects.

These include Canada's largest civil engineering project, the James Bay hydroelectric job, Saudi Arabia's Jubail Industrial City and New Zealand's natural gas-to-gasoline project.

The company's research and development section is one of the oldest and largest of its kind in the engineering and construction industry.

After his son, Riley, became president of the Bechtel Group in 1990, Steve Bechtel took on an advisory role. He serves as chairman of Bechtel Investments, Inc., and Sequoia Ventures, Inc., both separate but affiliated companies operating in real estate, natural resources and related fields.

Former President George Bush presented Steven Bechtel, Jr. the highest honor that can be bestowed on an American for technical achievement, the National Medal of Technology, in 1991.

Lodwrick Cook:
A Support System that Works

"We believe we have a responsibility and, in fact, it's in our best interests to be involved in the community in which we do business," says Lodwrick Cook, chairman and CEO of ARCO. "This involvement probably bears more mutual benefits to the community and ARCO if it's directed towards young people and education, and helps deal with some of the issues affecting minorities. MESA fits the bill quite admirably in touching base with all three of these areas of community involvement that we've selected for support."

Cook, a staunch supporter of MESA since 1978, served on the MESA Board of Directors and as chairman of the MESA Industry Advisory Board. Through his efforts, ARCO provided substantial financial support as well as a loaned executive who headed MESA's 920 financial drive which solidified industry's contribution to the program.

"We obviously can't be all things to everyone in trying to deal with the problems prevalent in today's society affecting the communities in which we do business," he says. "But we support MESA because it impacts our goals in being directed towards young people. It encourages all students, and certainly minority students, to stay in school and take math and science courses which relate to our business. MESA is unique in that potentially it helps feed recruits into our type of work. We need engineers, geophysicists, chemists and other technically trained personnel, more so than a lot of other businesses, so any program that produces recruits for us is in our own interest.

"There are other benefits from our involvement in these types of programs. We think the stability of the community is terribly important. This means society has to function in a stable sort of way that gives real hope and a future to its people. The cultural aspects of the community are important too, because they bind it together and provide the kind of climate that is conducive for harmony and progress. We, of course, have self interest in selling our products in a stable community, but in so doing we provide not only a service to the community but jobs as well.

"We encourage our employees to volunteer their services to programs such as MESA. We've got to do more than just throw cash at the problem. First of all we need feedback about what works best, and the best feedback is by having our own people involved. Also, we think they learn from it. They develop leadership skills and they learn how to get along with diversity in the community, and certainly our communities in California are becoming extremely diverse. The company doesn't make its money in isolation.

"Stability in the community is certainly in the best interest of our shareholders, to whom we are fully accountable. If the community goes up in flames, as it did recently in Los Angeles, it's not going to work too well for us. If we can help solve the problems that create the unrest, then obviously our business will prosper. If we can help create more affluent customers

Lodwrick Cook (center) with former President Jimmy Carter at gathering of Southern California students

—Photo fron ARCO photo collection

who like ARCO because of what they see us doing in the community, that's a good form of advertising too."

Commenting on the education system in this country, Cook makes the following observations: "We have probably the best higher education system in the world. But we're weak at the elementary and secondary school levels. That's why we've had to come up with MESA and related programs to help build a support system that wires around some of the inadequacies in the system. Obviously if the public school programs were working perfectly, we would have less need of a MESA. We would still need it because it provides students motivation that would ideally come from families. We still need the support MESA provides in the jump from high school to college. Presumably the public institutions could provide these services if they were perfect, but they aren't perfect. The system could certainly be a lot better, and that is what we are all trying to do."

Cook grew up in a small town in Louisiana. "There were five seniors in my high school graduating class and it was tough to be in the top 20 percent of that class. I always tell people I was third in my class and hope they never ask how big it was. I was active in youth organizations such as the 4-H Club. I went to summer camps and to fairs to show baby beef calves. I ended up being state president of the 4-H Club.

"There were many adults in my life who had a profound influence early on in terms of helping me focus on specific goals. It was just expected that I would go to college. It was quite clear higher education was the answer to breaking out of what was a dead-end future in a little country town that was losing its role of having an agricultural future. MESA is sort of like that. It helps kids break out of an uncertain future, providing a support system for them to stay in school and helping to bridge the transition from high school to university. I was lucky in that 4-H helped me in that regard because I had been at the university to show my baby beef calves and I knew the surroundings. They met me at the train early in the morning when I arrived, and took me out to the barn where I was provided with a room. That sounds kind of rough but actually it was one of the better rooms on the campus. I got all the free milk I could drink and I got my room free for doing some chores around the agricultural activity, even though I was not an agriculture student. After a year or so I moved on, but the experience gave me a base and a group of friends, a support system, if you will. MESA does that too. It takes kids from the inner city, provides a support system that helps the kids through college. So that's another reason why we're supportive of MESA. As I mentioned earlier, it fulfills the three areas that we think are important for us to work in: the educational field, young people, and minorities."

Dick Collins

Dick Collins: The Complete Convert

Richard M. Collins was probably the most important person in developing and crystallizing industry's involvement in the MESA partnership. As vice president and responsible officer for Bechtel's non-financial support services, including personnel, Collins was asked by Chairman Steve Bechtel, Jr. to look into the problem of meeting Affirmative Action/Equal Employment Opportunity guidelines relating to Bechtel's recruiting efforts. This started Collins' fourteen-year involvement in the MESA program.

"My association with MESA started in January 1978," he recalls. "Roger Heyns of the Hewlett Foundation called Steve Bechtel asking his help in forming a consortium of major engineering companies throughout the state to attack the problem of bringing more minorities into the engineering field. We were struggling to meet AA/EEO guidelines, which were particularly onerous for engineering firms since there were very few minority engineers or technicians available nationally.

"We saw AA/EEO as a band-aid solution to the problem which, obviously, like all social problems, demands a long-term solution. Steve Bechtel had been a charter member of the early Committee on Minorities in Engineering and he asked me to look at whether or not such a consortium could move us ahead in California, as contrasted to the national effort, which was making little progress.

"Ted Lobman, a senior staff officer of the Hewlett Foundation, told me about the MESA program at the University of California. I contacted Bob Finnell, who was executive director of the MESA program, and we met several times that March. These meetings acquainted me with MESA's goals and details of its program. I was impressed with Bob Finnell—his dedication and straightforward manner in answering every question I put to him. I liked the answers too. Everything about the program was pragmatic; it worked within the existing school systems involving principals, teachers, and parents; its emphasis was on the kids and their accomplishments; it provided recognition and incentives for the kids to achieve; it only targeted schools with large minority populations, in order to keep the odds in its favor; and it was both cost effective and results oriented.

"I became a complete convert and asked Finnell how industry could help. He suggested the formation of an Industry Advisory Board. It could provide policy guidance plus financial and in-kind aid to the program as well as field trips and summer employment opportunities for MESA students. This was the basic thrust of the 'game plan' we put together. I told Steve Bechtel we didn't need another organization and that it would be more sensible for California industry to support the existing MESA program. My argument for MESA was simply the logic of its basic premise—the way to get more minority engineers was to put more minority students in the pipeline.

"He bought my argument, and Finnell and I met with him on June 2. He agreed to call the CEO's of the thirteen major companies Finnell and I had identified, asking each one to become a charter member of the MESA Industry Advisory Board (IAB) and to appoint an officer-level individual to represent the firm on the board. All agreed and the IAB was off and running. Steve got even with me by telling the CEOs he had already had me appointed as the board chairman.

"Finnell asked me also to serve as a member of the Board of Directors of MESA. I attended the first meeting of the board at the Lawrence Hall of Science on September 28, 1978. Bill Somerton presided as temporary chairman of the historic meeting. Initial bylaws were adopted; Bill Somerton and Lee Browne were elected chairman and vice-chairman, respectively; the Industry Advisory Board was officially created and the proposed membership and company representatives were approved," says Collins, who worked for Bechtel thirty-five years in a number of engineering and management positions. He retired in 1985. Others in attendance at the first meeting were: Lee Browne, Tom Chinn, Rex Fortune, Gil Herrera, Ray Landis, Jaime Oaxaca, Robert Rice, Benito Sinclair, Mary Perry Smith and Mary Jane Wayne, secretary.

"I was privileged to continue to serve as IAB chairman three years and in that time I believe we accomplished our goal of increasing support for MESA. I credit several people in particular for their loyal attendance at board meetings and following through with their companies on behalf of MESA: Tom Tupper of Chevron, Tom Murphy of Fluor, and John Ball of Pacific Telephone. Lod Cook of ARCO succeeded me as chair in September 1981. He and Dennis Laurie put together Project 920 in 1983 which raised over $1 million for MESA and greatly expanded our industry support base.

"My work as chairman of the IBA was relatively easy because Finnell and I got together on the phone and decided on the meeting agenda. Bob put the staff work together and dropped by my San Francisco office to finalize it. Our meetings always went well. It was Bob's genius to always have MESA students and teachers at our board meetings to foster our enthusiasm.

"At one meeting a math teacher from a high school in Pomona stood up and thanked the board members for their support of MESA. 'I have been a math teacher for twelve years,' he said, 'and was so discouraged because I couldn't put a whole advanced math class together I had decided to give up teaching. Then MESA came into my school and now I teach two full trigonometry classes, and I wanted to thank you.'

"With a tear in my eye, I told him he didn't need to thank us but that we should thank him for staying on the firing line.

"At another meeting we had Glenn Seaborg as our guest. Halfway through the meeting, in walked Governor Jerry Brown and his whole entourage. He had gotten the word on MESA and it made a very good stop on his campaign trail. We got great press on the visit.

"Finnell's other genius was using all of his board members and IAB directors to the fullest extent to further the cause of MESA. I'm not sure that is still happening today. I recall writing many letters to the state legislators and others to gain support of MESA and I gave a number of talks in Sacramento and locally and a presentation to a National Convention of College Deans in Colorado.

"Finnell himself is one of the few persons I know who has the knowledge, demeanor, and vocabulary to be at home with members of all three of MESA's constituencies—academic, governmental, and industrial. More importantly, he realized the importance of the leverage each could provide. He knew what really registered with each of these constituencies. For example, he was supportive of my insistence on having a spread sheet showing actual and projected funding from various sources, number of facilities and students served versus expenditures, and a unit cost per student, to demonstrate MESA's cost efficiency. This 'bottom-line' approach impressed industry supporters," says Collins. A native of Brooklyn who graduated from New York City's Manhattan College, which presented him an award for academic achievement, Collins did his graduate work at Columbia University, specializing in Structural Engineering.

"A situation developed in early 1985 when the issue of MESA's governance came up as a result of the university restating restrictions on MESA's contacts with the state legislature. A faction advocated MESA disassociate itself from the university and become an independent entity. It proved a difficult time for Rex Fortune, chairman of the MESA board at that time, who as superintendent of the Inglewood Unified School District, was also going through a teachers' strike. Fortunately, I had retired from Bechtel the previous May. I had the time to do some leg work for Rex, putting together a presentation to argue against the move. We had a difficult board meeting to resolve the issue but our presentation carried the day due, in no small part, to the performance of Dr. Marjorie Gardner, who had just taken over as director of the Lawrence Hall of Science.

"After this board meeting, Bill Somerton and I put together a badly needed governance document. It served to put us back on the track where we stand today.

"So, as I look back on my fourteen years with MESA, I have many fond recollections of many accomplishments—though never enough—and wonderful personal relationships with special people like Bill Somerton, Mary Perry Smith, Bob Finnell, Ted Lobman, Lee Browne and Richard Santee from the early days; and all those that followed later—Marjorie Gardner, Fred Easter, Gene Cota-Robles, Tomas Arciniega, Stephanie McGraw, Gene Houston, Mary Ann Carr, Rod Hanks and many others.

"We have all been thrilled to see MESA grow in size, scope and quality such that it now truly provides that 'continuum' that we had envisioned at the outset. We can be proud of our association with a wonderful, successful program. It will continue to succeed because it is so right and its cause is so just."

Dick Collins is still a valued member of the MESA Board of Directors in 1992. He, like so many others, has "MESA fever" and can lay claim to part of the MESA magic.

Lawrence Baack: A Program that Should Be in Every School

In one of those story book coincidences, Lawrence Baack is a product of the school where the MESA program began. "I graduated from Oakland Tech in 1960 and when I came back to the Bay Area in 1980, MESA was up and running well."

Lawrence Baack (left) with California Assemblyman Tom Bates

—Photo by John Jernegan

The manager of Pacific Gas & Electric Company's Governmental Relations Department in San Francisco, Baack joined MESA in 1987, a year when the company was analyzing its contribution programs.

"A couple of areas really leaped out in the review," he says. "One was the work needed to keep young people in school so they could become self-sufficient. The second objective was to work on math and science SATs for young minority people. That was when we decided to pump up our support of MESA."

At a Southern California meeting he helped brainstorm PG&E's support for the MESA Advisors' Workshop idea. Baack assigned Tim Kelly as the company's first loaned executive and Kelly organized the first workshop at the company's San Ramon Learning Center. Baack's work on a state commission had revealed, "A lot of people cared about education...but they didn't value teachers. Teachers didn't perceive themselves to be underpaid; they perceived themselves to be undervalued by society. So I thought if we could have a first-class, but not ostentatious, event that would enable them to concentrate on the workshops, getting to know each other, having a team-building experience, they would know they're appreciated."

Baack's views on public education were shaped by good teachers all the way through the University of California, Berkeley, and Stanford University, where he obtained his doctorate. "My parents were good teachers; my neighbors were good teachers. You think about role models and caring adults—I was lucky because I had a lot of them."

Before attending Stanford he served for five years in the Navy, a hitch that included Vietnam duty. He taught at the University of Nebraska before returning to his roots. "My wife Jane was a school teacher. She got her doctorate and is a professor of business, at San Francisco State."

Math and science, he believes, can open doors for young people. "Success in those disciplines is, I think, the greatest chance for lasting opportunity for underrepresented minority students." It will be challenging in the Nineties, however. "I think resources will be more limited than they've been in the past," Baack says. "We're entering an era of limited resources. That means MESA must focus on maintaining excellent standards and producing good results. It means keeping administrative overhead low, running things in an efficient, effective way with the smallest possible utilization of funds.

"We have to continue telling the MESA story so it's even more successful in private fund raising; so MESA can go before the state legislature and fight for public dollars. The fact that MESA produces great results will not by itself ensure success." Budget cuts for police and mental health services, school closings, teacher salary cuts—these are among the problems that add to the challenge, says Baack, who chaired MESA's Advisory Board for two terms.

"Unless we're skilled in communicating the mission of MESA to all the key stakeholders and funders, broadening the circle of people who are supporters of

MESA, I think we're not going to be as successful in the Nineties. Which would be too bad, because it's an excellent program that should be in every school in this state with a sizeable number of minority students."

Mary Ann Carr: Earning Interest from Persistent Loans

When John Akers, retired IBM chairman of the board, checked out outstanding educational programs in the United States, the review included more than 200 undertakings. He chose MESA as one of the top ten.

"He was quite impressed," says Mary Ann Carr, K-12 Education Program manager in San Jose. "He thought it was exemplary in terms of

Mary Ann Carr

the student outcomes we were starting to see."

This explains why IBM in the past decade loaned thirty-five of its stellar performers to the MESA program in California. Each loaned executive represents a $100,000 per year contribution. In addition, the company has provided grants, upgraded MESA's research and evaluation equipment system, donated equipment, even sponsored a MESA Day egg-drop competition.

The annual $3,000 egg-drop gift reflects the ripple effect that strengthens MESA. "It was set up in 1986 while I was at Berkeley," says Carr. "The year I was there we went from sixteen employers contributing $16,000 to more than forty employers that gave about $70,000 in 1987 for MESA Day activities so kids could learn about careers."

The late Gene Houston worked with Professor Ray Landis during the development at California State University, Northridge of what is now called the MESA Minority Engineering Program, which helps underrepresented minorities cope with university level challenges.

Another IBM loaned executive, Lloyd Conaway, persisted with the California Assembly until it passed a bill that established a MESA program for junior high schools. He rounded up support of senior management from a number of companies in persuading legislators they should vote for the measure.

Ralph Rogers, while working with MESA's Kay Hudspeth at California Polytechnic State University in Pomona, convinced its School of Engineering to pay her salary, thus channeling an equivalent amount of MESA dollars into its program. It is an idea that has yet to catch on elsewhere.

Mary Ann Carr describes her two-year MESA stint as, "The best time of my life. I had been managing college recruiting. Lloyd Conaway was so impressed when he was up there he called me one day and said, 'I think it would be to IBM's benefit, and also to the benefit of MESA directors and students, if we hosted all the directors in the state for a two-day process.' On those two days we brought in two of our senior managers. They described our commitment to minority education. I brought my staff along, and we actually increased our minority representation by 13 percent with the summer students we brought in as a result of that effort."

She took Conaway's place when he returned to IBM. "I was impressed with the level of support from the senior managers of the companies participating in MESA. We worked closely with the vice presidents, and their dedication, their commitment, and their belief in these young people, who were going to be our future work force, was phenomenal.

"The directors I saw worked long hours, faced many challenges and struggled with financial constraints. Bottom line, it was always the students who kept them going despite all the dynamics of their jobs."

Carr still corresponds with some of the students she mentored. She led leadership workshops in Fresno and took part in MESA Day events in addition to her managerial role at the Statewide Office.

"When I came back, my job evolved and there was a tremendous interest in the company in K-12 education and its implications on our work force. Because of the MESA background, I had an opportunity to step into this position of program manager.

"We've done many things in supporting MESA. We've moved into collaborative efforts with other organizations to provide support in our communities. Some of our loaned executives helped when the MESA concept spread to Colorado and Washington, and some of them who served in California came from as far as New York to work on the program."

Chapter 9
California Gets Involved

By 1978 MESA's expansion had produced twelve centers in California. The first five-year plan guided the growth and the use of funds from the Hewlett and Sloan foundations. Member companies of MESA's Industry Advisory Board produced active volunteers from its member companies and some financial support. But the demand for MESA from high schools, the need for more services for participating students, and the five-year time limit on initial grants meant a successful long-term effort would require significant new support.

MESA's role at the University of California and California State University systems and private universities placed it in dramatic contrast to other programs providing college access to minority students. By 1977 the state was investing millions of dollars and staff members on each university campus were responsible for identifying, recruiting and providing students a variety of services. Minority enrollment had increased at California universities, both public and private, but cries came from minority groups, faculty, and elected officials, that few of these students graduated. Others lamented the low percentage of graduates in technical fields.

MESA's private source of funding and its focus on math-based fields of study did not duplicate existing state financed programs. Thus its board of directors and staff saw an opportunity to not only continue the program but promote its expansion as well, making an impact beyond the five-year life of the original Hewlett-Sloan grants. Their initial $1 million meant corporations and other foundations could buy into the MESA operation at a modest level without the risk of supporting a program with single-year funding. A company's support proved compatible with its interest in recruiting technically trained personnel while also serving the community. These concerns of companies in the late 1970s redounded to MESA's benefit. So MESA developed a strategy aimed at leveraging state resources with the private pledges for support. Since most programs ask for 100 percent funding from the state government, the board felt a matching-funds plan would please elected officials.

Exploratory talk began in 1979 midway in the California budget cycle. The Subcommittee on Education, chaired by John Vasconcellos, became interested in MESA's focus and its ability to bring private funds into an area generally ignored by minority education efforts. Bob Finnell, MESA's executive director, and others appeared before the subcommittee. At different points Assemblymen Vasconcellos, Peter Chacon, and Gary Hart began expressing support for MESA. Vasconcellos, who chaired the powerful Ways and Means Committee, later would gain public attention for starting a Self Esteem Committee at the state level.

Parallel inquiries from the California Postsecondary Education Committee (CPEC) and the Joint Legislative Budget Office arrived. Bruce Hamlett from CPEC prepared background reports on MESA as part of that agency's responsibility. At the same time Hal Geogue, John Woods and other budget office staffers reviewed MESA's program and budget, which showed that matching state support would speed the expansion pace and bring in more students.

"We need more industry support and participation in precollege education," legislators had said.

But in MESA's case they found themselves in a position of having ignored a major effort consistent with their desires for minority access, success in college and their support for a strong California technical base.

As MESA gained attention in Sacramento, directors of some other university programs sensed a potential rival. Most programs, fully funded by the university budget, focused on recruiting and delivering a variety of student services. These programs invested little in preparing students for their university level operations or doing follow-up studies of students so results could be measured. MESA's approach set in motion a whole new set of rules. Heated debates echoed in the corridors in Sacramento and university offices around the state. Because of the shift in thinking about secondary education that was to follow in the 1980s, the focus of the 1978-79 debates foreshadowed these major themes:

1. The role of the university in high school education.
2. Avoiding duplicate efforts.
3. The feasibility of paying students to achieve high grades.
4. How to measure private participation in education.

By setting entrance requirements, the university had in a sense set the agenda for high schools. But this shift toward investing in programs that prepared students for specific majors pointed in a new direction. Some educators endorsed it. Previously the university efforts merely recruited students, whether minority or not. But the facts showed most of the minority students could not major in more than 50 percent of university offerings because they lacked prerequisite courses, usually in math and science. Clearly, the nation, the professions and industry were losing a lot of the talent required in a competitive, technologically oriented society that required maximum use of its human potential. Individuals also ended up as losers. So, in the best interests of the state, more focused university involvement won hands down over a laissez-faire approach. MESA built heavily on this argument.

The charge that MESA duplicated other programs, while formidable, eventually turned to MESA's advantage. Campus recruiters targeted minority students by seeking high schools where they identified and eventually signed up students. Advocates of these programs cited their success in increasing minority enrollments on most university campuses. However, the MESA staff had analyzed enrollment, majors and graduation statistics of minority students. They showed these students did not pursue the spectrum of university majors and experienced a high dropout rate. Indeed, concerned campuses offered a variety of student and academic support services in an effort to retain minority students. However, these existing program implementers pursued their goals in a traditional way that never built a network that expanded their students' choices and preparation.

By focusing on preparing students for university enrollment so they could pursue its full range of offerings, MESA increased the chances they would graduate. By preparing students for maximum requirements, in contrast to the minimum requirements most minority students brought to their universities, MESA promised a needed infusion of technically skilled people in California's economy. The MESA approach also ensured that investments made in students would yield returns by increasing their chances of graduation. Preliminary data on the first MESA high schools revealed high college admission and attendance rates, a high choice of engineering and related majors, and a high persistence and success in initial courses. The challenge: to increase these numbers and demonstrate how expansion of the program through state investments would continue developing benefits. If they did not, then MESA lacked a case for continued state funding or, for that matter, any investment in the program from any source.

The most controversial part of the MESA program, one that received particular attention during legislative debates, was the incentive grants. From its inception, MESA paid modest sums, usually $400 a year, to students who made at least two A's and a B in their advanced math, science and English courses. This told students hard work produced rewards and gave them a goal they could achieve each semester. But to some the incentive grants smacked of rewarding students for doing what they were supposed to do.

"These awards are in the mainstream of American economic tradition— recognizing achievements with incentives," Bob Finnell, MESA's executive director, told legislators. "This is exactly what middle and upper class parents do for their students, except their awards are much higher than MESA's. Many of our students come from families with limited incomes. Their parents can't offer bonuses."

The awards also helped counter the pressure from high school students who scoffed at good grades and derided activities that deferred gratification.

All this debate proved ironic because in later years many others advocated incentive awards for students. The Cleveland Public School District's well publicized program in the early 1980s paid students for making high grades. Others followed suit. Some law makers never accepted the idea, but were mollified since private resources paid for more than half of MESA's program activities. This meant the state would not be fully funding the incentive awards.

Finally, MESA fielded questions about verifying its matching private funds and using the University of California as a vehicle to disburse funds to outside universities. A related question dealt with the reserve funds MESA annually carried over to guarantee program continuity.

"We kept detailed financial accounts separately, so I could show our reserve fund came from private sources," Finnell recalls. "I suggested an audit could verify that MESA received private funding." He told the legislators, "The reserve fund would let us pay for programs until we received matching state money."

"Why do you need state funding with your reserve of several hundred thousand dollars?" budget analysts asked.

Based on the legislators' logic, only when all funds are committed or spent is state funding required. Finnell explained the fiscal realities preferred by local school districts where government funding often arrived late and supported revolving door programs. Principals, after being hounded to accept programs funded for one, two, or three years, often discovered funds had evaporated by the time programs showed results.

MESA's founders and board members avoided that cycle. They designed a five-year effort with a reduced start-up year that built up a program reserve.

"Thus we could promise principals, teachers, and students a five-year minimum life cycle and we were optimistic about continuing for years ahead," Finnell says. "As we received more industry contributions, our credibility with educators increased. After they saw the reserve, they recognized we just might not be a revolving door project. The reserve gave us at least a one or two-year cushion just in case it was necessary before closing down a MESA center or a school site.

Perhaps because of our adamant views, the reserve fund survived."

Legislators, legislative analysts and budget staff members during late 1978 and early 1979 requested information or handled tasks related to the state budget allocation proposed for MESA. The first MESA allocation request came after university budgets had been submitted. So when Subcommittee on Education members heard testimony on university budgets, Finnell was asked for comments. MESA's principal investigator, Professor Wilbur Somerton, and its associate director, Mary Perry Smith, also answered legislators' questions.

Finnell set up MESA's first board meeting in Sacramento where legislative staffers watched its leadership in action. Guests at the April 5, 1979 meeting also included representatives from the California State Department of Education and other agencies. MESA board member Thomas Chinn, a Sacramento school board member and associate architect of the state, hosted the meeting. Later it became an annual Sacramento event, where state officials could meet face to face with MESA's multi-sector board. The visitors could see the broad base of support for MESA and gauge how much money industry and foundations would contribute if the California legislation authorized matching grants.

During the first MESA board meeting a legislative aide expressed some skepticism about the depth of support and reasons for preparing minority students for, in his eyes, the extremely difficult field of engineering. At that point Richard Collins, a Bechtel vice president and the head of MESA's Industry Advisory Board, described his engineering career. It had taken him all over the world, he said, as he worked on major construction projects, building power plants, visiting refineries and mines, and meeting people and seeing places he had only read about growing up in the Bronx in New York. The field offered a career full of accomplishment and romance that brought an engineer excitement and challenges. For Collins, it was both emotionally fulfilling and intellectually challenging.

"I want to be sure minority youth have the same opportunity for that kind of excitement," he said. "I want them to design and build projects vital to human life."

His statement, unlike the arid arguments or statistics often heard in debates, made a profound impression on everyone at the meeting that day.

Budget items ground ahead in Sacramento toward the June 30 budget approval deadline. So through the spring of 1979 MESA's appropriation moved toward reality. In one climactic session a subcommittee member moved that MESA be allocated $250,000. In a brief discussion that followed, another member even proposed adding some more funds. But Finnell said the initial three-year expansion has been thought out and additional funds would hinder rather than help. With the subcommittee's approval, it became only a matter of time for the Assembly Ways and Means Committee, the Senate, and finally the Governor to sign the measure.

The state's allocation of $250,000 for 1979-80 became a milestone, comparable to the initial Hewlett/Sloan expansion grant, in moving the program ahead. Its key provision of matching state funds one-to-one with private funds provided MESA with leveraging of private industry so increased levels of private support would be available. It also increased the chances of an annual state allocation.

That became the case. By 1991 MESA had received a total of $10 million from the state for its program. The modest beginning level of private funding over the years increased to $700,000 a year. Additional foundations, impressed by the program that was in place, began investing. They felt confident that the extensive MESA network would ensure success. With state funding, MESA boosted its number of centers to fifteen by the early 1980s and eighteen centers by 1991. From the nearly 1,500 students it served by the end of its first five years, MESA was serving 3,000 high school students during 1991.

California funds invigorated a program that possessed three characteristics surfacing in the national educational debate that erupted in the late 1980s and early 1990s:

A focus on high school math and science.

A recognition that preparing minority students for careers in engineering and other math-related fields was vital for the economy, the professions and the country.

A substantial use of volunteers and resources from the private sector.

MESA then built on the 1979 state funding by proposing a university engineering retention program in 1982. As early as 1978 MESA sponsored a workshop on "The Retention of Minority Students in Engineering." Its purpose: to analyze and improve retention rates for minorities underrepresented in the engineering professions. The workshop, co-sponsored by the Committee on Minorities in Engineering and the National Research Council, recognized minority students still needed a variety of supportive services that helped them persist and graduate. More than fifty representatives from industry, universities, and other institutions attended the workshop, setting the stage for MESA's second effort to secure state funds for its work.

A plan, approved by the MESA board of directors in early 1981, led to a proposal for establishing ten university level retention programs based on the model developed at CSU Northridge under Professor Raymond Landis. For a period in early 1981, Mike Macias, National Action Council for Minorities in Engineering's West Coast program officer, was loaned to assist MESA in generating the program proposal. After various reviews and revisions, a proposal went to the appropriate state budget committees to start a MESA Minority Engineering Program at ten California engineering schools at a cost of $400,000.

Probably because of MESA's initial success and the use of state resources in that effort, acceptance of the second university program went smoothly. In fact, Sacramento legislators provided funding for twelve centers. These allocations, renewed annually, totalled almost $5 million by 1991.

Continued funding of both MESA's high school and university programs resulted in part from external evaluations. They documented the achievements of MESA students. UCLA's Center for the Study of Evaluation and the CPEC both produced studies that led to continued funding of MESA. These evaluations also provided industry and foundations with data that demonstrated their grants, leveraged by the state funds on either a one-to-one or one-to-two basis, produced the results expected.

MESA's initiatives and cooperation with the state and its universities had by 1991 produced nearly $16 million in financial support. With matching corporate and foundation funding and in-kind contributions, MESA reached a strong financial base for its long-term effort of altering the output of technical talent in the state. Far from a "Mom and Pop" or crisis-oriented operation that disappeared the week after the media hype, MESA achieved credibility among educators and parents, attracted a competent staff and received attention for addressing a significant educational challenge in a variety of educational settings because of adequate funding. It did so without stacking the cards in its favor by concentrating in areas where success would be expected. Instead, MESA took its model into the most challenging high schools, delivered its service with the help of volunteers, and produced successful graduates in numbers that far exceeded expectations.

Teresa Hughes:
Discovering Where the Policy Is Made

One of the most significant events since MESA began in 1970 is the passage of California Assembly Bill 610, the so-called Hughes bill. Passed by the Assembly in February 1985, then by the Senate, and signed into law by the governor, the bill codifies the goals and structure of MESA and makes it a line item in the state budget. MESA owes a debt of gratitude to Dr. Teresa Hughes for sponsoring, promoting and steering this bill through the state legislature.

A low-key representative of a south central Los Angeles district, which in 1993 was California's poorest, Hughes has led the way on educational and health care bills since her election in 1975. MESA, she says, is "...extremely important. I feel it is important for anyone to be inspired by a discipline at an

Assemblywoman Teresa Hughes presents Fred Easter —Photo by John Jernegan
with a special state assembly resolution to honor MESA

early age so that this can be part of their lifetime ambitions and goals. That's one of the things greatly lacking in our public education system today. Because of various family structures and broken families, young people are not encouraged early enough. As I go around and speak to different professionals, they tell me they always wanted to be what they are today. That's why I feel MESA is very much needed in this day and age when we are a society of high technology. It gives that early motivation and access to academic experiences and interests. I think it's an absolutely marvelous program and I'm very proud of it."

Hughes, a New York City native, attended Hunter College, receiving a bachelor's degree in physiology and public health. She says she is fascinated by bioscience. Her two graduate degrees were in education administration—a master's degree from New York University and a Ph.D. from Claremont Graduate School. She has been a social worker, teacher, school administrator, and professor of education at California State University, Los Angeles. Her husband, Dr. Frank E. Staggers, was president of the National Medical Association, which is made up of African-American physicians.

"As an educator I thought policy was made at the university level, but after teaching at a university, I found out the real policy was made at the state legislative level. That's how I became interested in running for public office. I wanted to make a difference and I think I have."

Hughes has been reelected repeatedly and was unopposed in 1990. She chaired the Education Committee of the assembly from 1982 to 1990 and headed the Health and Human Services Subcommittee. She easily won a race for state senate in 1992.

She's made a difference by authoring a bill that created the Math and Science Academy at CSU Dominguez Hills. A math/science magnet school in Los

Angeles is named for her. At first the school was to have been a performing arts magnet, but Hughes said, "No, these children really need an experience with math and science." She is also delighted that the Museum of Science and Industry is in her district.

"I represent a poor working-class community very much like the community I grew up in—an ethnically diverse community that needed to provide opportunities for people to get a good education, a good foundation, and to have opportunities to go on for higher education," she says. "That's the platform I ran on and that's how I won in a field of ten or twelve people."

Her district included 47.3 percent Hispanic and 39.9 percent African-Americans in 1992.

In view of the state's budget crisis in that year, she says, "I think it's going to be absolutely critical that business and industry reinvest in education because it's to their benefit to do so. They need competent workers who can move up to the corporate level. They can't just go to a university and say, 'These are the people we need.' It has to start early, just like the MESA program starts early on, inspiring and interesting young people in math and science fields. So I think corporate America must do more reinvestment in our youth."

Bruce Hamlett:
The Case for Quality Control

"In California, within the budgetary process, MESA is now perceived to be one of the most effective programs of this type by folks within the Department of Finance, by folks in the capitol," says Dr. Bruce Hamlett. As associate director of the Sacramento-based California Postsecondary Education Commission, he helped advise state legislators on educational trends and problems until becoming executive director of the New Mexico Commission on Higher Education in 1993.

What keeps MESA honest?

"I think first of all was the requirement that any state dollars, public money, be matched by private-sector dollars. The dollar-for-dollar match assures that private dollars come in and it's our assumption the private sector is much more likely to be concerned with accountability and effectiveness than the public sector is, and that's one key check. The second key check would be the advisory board that the MESA program has, that includes not only public institutional representatives but also folks from the private corporate sector. Again, that's sort of an oversight process and layering, protecting and promoting quality. The third is the leadership of the MESA staff itself, the expressed

Bruce Hamlett   —Photo by The Photography
                                   Studio, Sata Fe, NM

commitment to deal with outcomes and to publish outcome data as is included in the annual report."

Regarding the background of government support for programs affecting minorities, Hamlett says, "In the late Sixties and early Seventies, when there was a response to civil disobedience, it was a decision by President Johnson at the federal level, as well as at the state level, to put a lot of money into equity programs. Looking back, I don't think we had a good sense of what effective strategies would be, but a lot of money was thrown at the problem. Now in the Nineties, based on our experience with MESA as well as several other programs, we now have a pretty good base of knowledge about the strategies that help keep kids in school, to keep them on the academic college prep track, and get them into certain disciplines. We know what will work. The difference between now and the Seventies and late Sixties is that now there doesn't seem to be a public will or a political commitment to invest in the implementation of these programs. So the problems are greater now in the inner cities than they were, certainly, in the Seventies. The will to put resources into solutions just isn't there."

CPEC conducted evaluations of the MESA program that included helpful suggestions. "We were directed by the legislature to do an assessment of all the outreach programs, including MESA; eight programs in all," says Hamlett. "What I tried to do was to put together on a chart various indicators of success and indicators of useful components of the programs and indicate whether the programs did them or not. MESA pretty much had all the 'yeses' in the places where there should be 'yeses.' Most of the other programs did not. The cumulative effect is that the people in the capitol now appreciate and look for these outcome data, and because of them, MESA has been successful in getting more money when it has been asked for. It hasn't always been asked for but, when it's been asked for, it's usually been responded to in an affirmative way."

When asked about the resolution passed by the state legislature mandating expansion of MESA-like programs to all schools in the state with 40 percent or more minority enrollment, Hamlett responded, "Legislation we sponsored a couple of years ago asked the various programs, including MESA, to come up with a strategy to move them from where they are now on a pilot phase serving a limited number of schools, to a full statewide operation. How do you do it? How much money do you need to do it? Responses are now coming in to CPEC and later this year we'll be coming up with a report that pulls them all together and offers our recommendations for full expansion. The problem is the fiscal condition of the state and the lack of will to raise additional revenues to fund these programs. But they work. We know they work. And we know why they work. There are quality control measures in place for MESA, so if there is a way to get additional money, it will be provided."

Hamlett has reservations about expansion of MESA to lower grade levels (K-6). He believes that MESA should continue to do what it does best. His first priority for expansion would be to offer MESA services to all 7-12 students who could be eligible for those services. His second priority would be for expansion of MESA and college-level MESA Program services to all Mexican-American, African-American and Native-American students who enter college and want to study math, engineering, or science. The third priority, later on, would be K-6. That's because K-6 doesn't lend itself so much to a disciplined, specific kind of approach. A different approach would be needed from what MESA does so well now. In addition, the payoff period, i.e., assessing the success of a K-6 program, would be ten years or more.

Hamlett also has reservations about expansion of the program into community colleges. "Other agencies, such as community colleges, have begun to request money through the budget process so that they can set up MESA programs," he says. "It's sort of like, 'It's now seen as a good thing. Let's buy into the action.' It's not clear that they have the capacity to run effective programs." Others would argue with this point of view, but clearly a strong case would have to be made to get CPEC's approval of such an expansion.

"When programs stop their narrow focus and begin to get broader and broader, they get diluted in their effectiveness," Hamlett says. "I think they need to focus, just do that limited task outstandingly and not try to do more things. Make sure that everyone who ought to know or has reason to know hears about MESA's success."

As for the future of education in California, Hamlett says, "I think the strategies that make MESA successful are generic kinds of things that could be applied to all students generally, in various other career areas, both at the 7-12 level and at the collegiate level. Ideally, the best way is not to have a MESA but to have each and every school and each and every student exposed to and have the benefits of the kinds of services MESA provides. Ideally, the school should be doing what MESA's doing without need for a special program."

Students from Tranquility High School observing livestock at Cal Poly San Luis Obispo

Chapter 10
Opting for Growth

If a seer had told MESA's founders in its early days that twenty-two years later the program would be serving nearly 14,000 students in California alone, they would have been amazed. Early expansion from 1971-1976 included a junior high school, then two more high schools.

"This to us was a major accomplishment," says Bill Somerton, a co-founder and a retired University of California, Berkeley engineering professor.

The idea of growing from one center with three high schools to ten centers serving twenty-five high schools in one year seemed impossible to the early visionaries. "We worried about it threatening the quality of the program," he says. The successful growth by 1992 to twenty pre-college centers, twenty-six college-level programs and seven "Success Through Collaboration" sites showed the worries were unfounded.

MESA Minority Engineering Program

By 1982, fifteen pre-college MESA centers served 104 high schools in California. They graduated 748 students who met MESA graduation require-ments. Almost 90 percent of them attended four-year universities and colleges with better math know-how and college survival skills than non-MESA minority youth. Still they could use continuing support in their college-level courses. In the early Seventies Professor Ray Landis at California State University, Northridge began developing an academic support program that provided assistance to underrepresented minority students majoring in engineering. It was called the Minority Engineering Program and it later became the model for the MESA Minority Engineering Program (MESA MEP). In 1982, the California State

Legislature appropriated funds to establish twelve MESA MEP programs on University of California and California State University campuses. The program focused on increasing the retention rates of underrepresented minority students majoring in engineering.

MESA MEP resembled the pre-college MESA program. The targeted group included MESA participants as well as other underrepresented minority group students already enrolled in an engineering program. Students in the program receive these fundamental services:

1. **Recruitment and admissions**. MESA MEP staff helps pre-college students complete college application forms, provides orientation, assists in selecting courses, and furnishes related services.

2. **Matriculation**. Once a student applies to the university, MESA MEP staff assists the individual in applying for financial aid, relevant scholarships, housing, registering for required placement tests, and other transition needs.

3. **Freshman year transition**. Participants receive a structured freshman year transition program consisting of (a) orientation and adjustment to the institution's environment, (b) study skills training, (c) monitoring student progress, and (d) motivation and career awareness training.

4. **Counseling**. Participants benefit from academic advice and personal counseling provided by peers and professional mentors.

5. **Student study center**. Each university program provides a study center for participants. It houses additional texts and other educational resources, and provides space for supervised student study groups and tutorial programs.

6. **Career development and summer job placement**. Students attend special career seminars and get opportunities to work in the summer at participating industries and businesses.

7. **Financial aid**. Besides assisting participants apply for financial aid, MESA MEP staff generates special financial aid and scholarships specifically for MESA MEP students.

8. **Student organizations**. Popular and scientific literature agree that thematic student groups assist in the retention of students. The MESA MEP component (a) lends resources to already established student organizations, and (b) helps initiate student clubs that focus on math, science, and engineering themes.

The MESA MEP program operated out of MESA headquarters in the Lawrence Hall of Science. Gene Houston, a loaned executive from IBM, was responsible for setting the program in place in 1982-83. Robert Finnell, then executive director of MESA, said of Houston's involvement, "In the months since he joined

us, Gene has imple-
mented our statewide
MESA MEP effort. He
participated in every
phase of our startup,
including preparing
proposal guidelines,
reviewing funding re-
quests from universi-
ties, assisting in in-
terviewing staff, and
training the twelve-
person MESA MEP
team. In addition, he
completed numerous

Teaching about science

campus site visits and
provided assistance to the engineering schools and MESA MEP staff. Needless
to say, Gene's role has been key to our ability to make the MEP program
operational on a statewide basis this past year."

Only three years after initiation of the state mandated MESA MEP program
the California Legislature directed the California Postsecondary Education
Commission (CPEC) to assess the impact of MESA MEP in reducing attrition
rates among minority engineering students. In December 1986 CPEC released
report 86-33, "Retention of Students in Engineering," which found:

1. Before 1982, when MESA MEP was established, retention rates for
   African-American and Mexican-American engineering students on UC
   campuses were 59 percent and 51 percent, respectively, after two years
   of study. This compared with 70 and 65 percent, respectively, for
   African-American and Mexican-American students in MESA MEP for
   a comparable period.
2. Among **all** freshmen who entered UC in engineering in 1982, 47 percent
   were still enrolled after three years. In comparison, 60 percent of MESA
   MEP students remained.
3. Comparative retention rates are the most striking within MESA's target
   ethnic groups at UC. Sixty-four percent of African American MESA
   MEP participants continued in engineering after three years, compared
   with 13 percent of non-MESA MEP participants. Among Mexican
   American students, 57 percent of MESA MEP students continued,
   compared with only 21 percent of non-participants.
4. Data for California State Universities indicate similar trends.

Junior MESA leadership conference at Cal Poly San Luis Obispo —Photo by David Ball

CPEC found program quality variations at some centers, attributable for the most part to the embryonic stage of development and local glitches. Nevertheless, CPEC cited several MESA MEP components for effectively retaining minority engineering students, including:

1. **Sense of community**. Freshman orientation, clustering students in freshman math and science classes, and the MESA MEP study center idea helped unify the young men and women.
2. **Academic support**. This includes intensive academic workshops focused on MESA MEP math and science courses (modeled on the Professional Development Program developed by Dr. Uri Triesman at UC Berkeley). Tutoring, study skills training and academic advising also contribute.
3. **Professional and personal support**. MESA MEP students are encouraged to join campus chapters of minority engineering societies. Summer jobs, internships, and career awareness activities further develop interpersonal and leadership skills, and build confidence.
4. **Disciplinary base**. MESA MEP centers are located in, and considered part of, the engineering school. This directly involves faculty members as academic advisors.
5. **Emphasis on student-to-student interaction**. Group interaction, rooted in common academic goals, improves understanding and mastery of

course materials, and builds confidence through group problem solving.

6. **Specialized recruitment.** MESA MEP staff recruits at the high school and college levels, using a variety of strategies. In addition, these students assume responsibility for encouraging pre-college students to become involved in engineering and in MESA MEP.

"Success of the existing program warrants its expansion to all public universities and its availability to all interested minority students in engineering," CPEC recommended.

Later studies on MESA MEP accomplishments by impartial bodies echoed this finding. The most recent figures showed 23 MESA MEP centers in California, serving nearly 5,000 students. A combining of NACME statistics (see Appendix X) with MESA statistics (see Appendix XI) shows that over 90 per cent of the underrepresented minority graduates in California had participated in MESA MEP.

Out-of-State Expansion

MESA's reputation was enhanced by evaluations by CPEC and other evaluators, as well as exposure in national forums. Other states inquired about replicating the program. As early as 1973, a representative of Johns Hopkins University visited Berkeley, investigating the fledgling program. This led to the formation of the first out-of-state offspring, known as MESA Baltimore.

In 1982 MESA Statewide staff met with representatives of Colorado, New Mexico, Texas, Arizona, and Washington, discussing possible replication. MESA designed these meetings to ensure that any replication would adhere to the original model in its most significant dimensions, e.g., local leadership, an academic setting, matching funds, promoting academic excellence, fostering efficiency and effectiveness.

California MESA leaders had always sought to ensure the program neither duplicated nor supplanted existing efforts. When MESA staff members visited sites, they insisted that the introduction of the MESA model would result in enhancing local resources and initiatives. These out-of-state expansion efforts could serve as a pilot test of a MESA expansion system package. This underscored the importance of determining that the proposed sites were indeed suitable for MESA programs. As a result of these and other informational sessions, Colorado, New Mexico, and Washington submitted proposals to MESA for replication funding.

With financial support from the William and Flora Hewlett Foundation in 1982, MESA awarded representatives of the three states with $25,000 each per year for a maximum of three years. This seed money helped the three states generate enough funds from universities, school districts, and industries to launch full-fledged MESA-type programs. They soon became successful.

Since those early days, twelve more states started MESA-type programs. MESA California provided staff training for many of these. These programs are listed in Appendix XII. The programs developed in their own way in order to adjust to meet local conditions. By and large, they adhered to the basic MESA model. Students throughout the country were benefiting from the services that MESA-type programs provide at the close of 1992.

Junior MESA

"In MESA's first years, we saw it was necessary to include junior high schools in the program if we were to encourage more students to enter math-based university tracks," says Somerton. "At first, Mary Perry Smith selected her Oakland Technical High students enrolled in geometry, which has first-year algebra 1 as a prerequisite."

Oakland Tech, at that time, was only a three-year high school, so algebra was usually taken in feeder junior high schools. Smith recognized this situation and requested Woodrow Wilson Junior High, the main feeder junior high into Tech, become part of the program. Thus, the first expansion of the program was to include a junior high.

After the statewide expansion of the program, several of the new centers adopted junior high or middle schools that fed into their MESA high schools. Lacking statewide funding for these schools, centers had to generate their own funds. However, their inclusion was so impelling, a MESA task force was set up to study junior high expansion. In 1983 Carnegie Foundation provided a grant for a pilot junior high program. Programs began at UC Berkeley, University of Southern California, and California State University, Long Beach. Based on their experiences, the task force developed a set of guidelines for a full-fledged Junior MESA program.

"Without appropriate preparation at the junior high school level, many students are precluded from either participating fully in MESA high school programs or graduating from high school with sufficient academic preparation in math, science, and English to be eligible to enter college on a regular basis and pursue a math/science-based career," the guidelines began. The structure and philosophy of MESA lends itself naturally to the development of a junior high school component. Early intervention increases the number of eligible students in high schools and eventually in universities. Extending the MESA philosophy and structure down into middle and junior high school level, with some modifications, creates a continuum which allows MESA to influence students from sixth grade through high school and to graduation from college, the task force said.

The Junior MESA program model closely resembles the high school program. In 1985, the California legislature passed Assembly Bill 610. It not only established MESA in California statute (Education Code Sections 8612-8618), but also provided for the development and funding of Junior MESA. The bill mandates that:

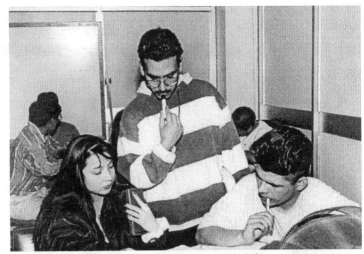

Cal Poly Pomona's MEP Academic Excellence Workshop

> ...the MESA program shall develop a model comprehensive engineering and career preparatory program designed to increase junior high school pupils' awareness of, and preparation for, career options in engineering and science. The objectives of the program shall be all of the following:
> (a) To increase the pool of low-income and ethnic-minority students who complete junior high school prepared to embark upon a college preparatory high school program which includes four years of coursework in mathematics, English, and science, respectively.
> (b) To increase the number of low-income and ethnic-minority junior high school students who complete pre-algebra and pre-geometry courses.
> (c) To enhance the content and consistency of general mathematics and science in junior high school curricula.
> (d) To provide junior high school teachers with in-service and other training opportunities which improve the quality of their instruction and interaction with students.

Funding for the Junior MESA program required matching funds (on a one-for-one basis) from the private sector. A grant from Carnegie Foundation provided the match funds and the Junior MESA program was initiated in 1985. By 1992-93, 95 junior high schools with nearly 4,000 students participated in the program.

Assembly Bill 610 further mandated CPEC to evaluate the effectiveness of the Junior MESA program and submit a report summarizing the evaluation and making recommendations regarding the merits of the program. CPEC Report 89-

Tug-of-war during Junior MESA Academy at Bishop

30 entitled, "Evaluation of the Junior MESA Program" was published in October 1989. Its conclusions include:

Junior MESA has had significant positive impact on participating students, as measured by their course selections, career planning, and aspirations for higher education. Students identified the program as important in peer support and individual encouragement. Further, Junior MESA is perceived to have a very positive effect on the senior high MESA component.

The operational requirements established for Junior MESA have served as effective guideposts for the development, maintenance, and improvement of the individual projects. MESA field trips, curriculum enrichment, and the competitions associated with MESA Day are valued by students, advisors, and center directors.

Although the program is viewed as being effective overall, there is considerable unevenness among various centers in terms of activities, and number of students, schools, and districts participating in the program. There is need for enhanced attention to the staffing and budgetary requirements for Junior MESA that fosters centers' flexibility to respond effectively to local needs and exigencies.

Parents, although not extensively involved, exhibit more interest in school and their students' progress as a result of the program.

Innovative and exemplary practices and activities are being implemented in Junior MESA at individual centers. These need to be identified and shared among center directors. School and district personnel are not as aware of the program and its impact as they should be.

The CPEC report recommended that, given its effectiveness, Junior MESA should be continued and expanded.

Community College Involvement

Extended discussions between MESA leaders and community college administrators in 1992 showed that some community colleges were interested in participating in the MESA network of programs. These colleges prepare interested students for admission to four-year colleges or universities. Some observers felt standards were lowered when students attended community colleges before entering technical or scientific fields of study at the upper division university level. There is a large number of students who attend high schools that do not have a MESA program. About 85 percent of the underrepresented students who go on to post-secondary institutions enroll in a community college. Many of them lack the rigorous academic preparation MESA provides. Others missed junior high school counseling that would have put them on the math-based academic track; they then fell too far behind to catch up in high school. Some MESA students bloom late because they do not achieve the grade point average needed to qualify for enrollment in a major four-year institution. Although many MESA students receive college scholarships and other financial aid, some students do not and must attend community colleges because of personal and financial reasons.

Several MESA MEP centers on their own have provided some MESA-type support to local community colleges encouraging qualified students to enter engineering programs as juniors. UC officials encourage campuses to admit qualified community college transfer students as a means of dealing with overcrowding. Statistics show qualified community college transfers perform as well as their four-year counterparts. Fred Easter, executive director of California Statewide MESA, says community colleges provide a filtering mechanism, helping assure the success of qualified transfer students. Easter believes admission of community colleges to the MESA MEP program is the wave of the future.

"If we can increase the number of students who come to us from community colleges, we will increase the number of students who graduate with degrees in engineering in the shortest possible time," he says.

Problems exist with community college expansion, he admits. There is value in the MESA model if it is fully implemented, but not all institutions see it that way. Some out-of-state programs, for example, want the name, then adjust it to what they see as the uniqueness of the local situation. This does not pose a problem except when they do the easy things but sluff off the things that are more difficult.

"We are not yet in the position of being able to shower them with money and obtain the leverage that goes with it," Easter says. "We have established a licensing document that enables us to enter into agreements with institutions where money is not changing hands and that is going to make it somewhat easier to expand the MESA concept nationwide. The point is, however, that managing the growth and expansion of the model into the community college system is a major effort."

In California there are nearly 100 community colleges and they enroll more than eight out of ten of MESA's targeted population who go on to post-secondary institutions.

Success Through Collaboration Program

Another example of how MESA concepts can be adapted to different situations is the Success Through Collaboration (STC) program that started early in 1992. Teri Lee, MESA's public relations director, describes this new thrust in a report as follows:

> ...focuses on increasing the number of Native-American students who successfully graduate from college with degrees in math- and science-based fields. It provides academic support through its partnership with American Indian centers, educators, tribal leaders, state officials, industry, and MESA personnel.
>
> STC operates in seven California sites and reaches some 200 students, many of whom live on reservations and rancherias. It offers academic advice, teacher training, field trips, and guest speakers stimulating student interest in math and science. The program mainly targets junior high school age youth.
>
> One of STC's most successful activities has been the introduction of MESA academies. These engage students in hands-on activities such as construction of straw towers, and building and launching model rockets. Academy activities also include traditional Indian concerns such as preservation of the environment and respect for nature.
>
> Plans call for developing non-remedial enrichment curricula from kindergarten through college. These will incorporate American Indian professional role models and Indian cultural activities, and highlight Indian contributions in math and science.
>
> The key to the project's success is the collaboration between Indian center directors and MESA.
>
> "Most of the STC center educators are members of the community," says Dolores Terrell, STC director. "They bring in their sensitivity to the needs of American Indian students. MESA brings in the MESA model, industry involvement, and its years of affiliation with universities. It's a perfect combination."
>
> A grant from California Department of Energy's Energy Extension Services helped fund staff positions. Staff members traveled to Lawrence Livermore Laboratory for an extensive training session on its Cray

supercomputer. PG&E provided lodging for the participants. Caltrans, the first STC site sponsor, underwrites the Owens Valley program.

Lee's report also mentions one participant:

> Mark Temple, a 19-year-old Micmac Indian, had never thought about becoming an engineer until he encountered the STC program. Just out of high school, Temple tutored elementary school students at the Bishop Indian Education Center when he attended the first MESA Academy. Later, excited by an STC-sponsored visit to the Lawrence Livermore Laboratory, Temple made his decision. He would continue his education and become an engineer.
>
> Today Temple attends Cerro Coso Community College. He now works as a student engineering assistant with Caltrans, where he conducts pre-building materials testing. Temple hopes he'll become a civil engineer.
>
> "I had always hated math and science," he says, "but MESA made me look at them in a different way. I never thought of going into engineering until MESA came and explained it to me."

The Effort Pays Off

Appendices VI through VIII show, respectively, freshmen and total undergraduate enrollments and B.S. degrees granted underrepresented minority engineering students in U.S. universities for the 1973-93 period. Nearly 250 per cent growth in the number of graduates and 300 per cent growth in students entering the field are encouraging. Appendices IX and X show freshmen enrollment and engineering graduates for California. Freshmen enrollment increased over 500 per cent while the underrepresented minorities receiving B.S. degrees reached 10.5 per cent of the total degrees granted engineering students in California, compared to 7.95 per cent for the U.S. as a whole.

Overall growth of the MESA program, following statewide expansion in 1977, is summerized in Appendix XI. The bottom lines on the table show an alarming decrease in MESA California expenditure per student. This is a consequence of an increase in the number of students admitted to the programs without a corresponding increase in available funds. Although this decrease in funding from MESA California is made up in part by local MESA center-generated funds, services to students have had to be cut with the inevitable consequence of some decrease in quality of the program. Pressures of the continued demand to expand the program create problems that need to be called to the attention of educators, state legislators, and the business community.

Richard Hart:
Another Approach to Expansion

"Years ago I left the university, where I was dividing my time between teaching and research, to go to Cabrillo Community College where I could be involved in full-time teaching, which is what I had always wanted to do," says Rich Hart. "I left being a highly specialized petroleum engineer to become a broad generalist lower-division engineering educator. My students have gone on to four-year schools in California and proceeded to graduate with degrees in engineering and are out there in the workplace. So it's been a gratifying experience."

Cabrillo Community College in Santa Cruz, California, has a MESA Center which works with a local high school, a middle school and, some day soon, Hart hopes, a MESA program for Cabrillo Community College students. He is active with the California Engineering Liaison Committee, a group that arranges a smooth flow of students between segments of the post-secondary education system. He emphasizes that it reports the number of students who start their engineering careers at community colleges has steadily increased to nearly 50 percent in 1992. The emphasis in MESA has been to get students into four-year colleges and universities. As a consequence, many well-qualified community college students are denied the benefits of MESA MEP.

Many outstanding students attend community colleges for a variety of reasons, he says. The financial advantage, especially in difficult economic times, is obvious. Classes are smaller and students receive more individual attention. There are sociological advantages too, particularly among the Hispanic community; many families are not ready for their children to leave home for college when they graduate from high school.

Hart would like community colleges to replicate the high school MESA model rather than the university level MESA Minority Engineering Program, which as the name reflects, is limited to engineering students. Community college math and science majors also need the advantages of a MESA program, he maintains.

Richard Hart with student

Cabrillo received a grant from the California Community College Chancellor's Office for developing a program similar to MESA. "It allowed us to expand and explore a tutorial program we had developed earlier," Hart says. "We managed to make that grant money last a year and a half but it was not renewed. So, they gave us seed money, we planted a seed, we got a nice sprout, but then they cut us off." Salvaged from the short-lived program was a report on how to implement a MESA program for community college students.

Hart is encouraged by MESA's initiative in starting a community college program. "We're going ahead without the money," he says. "We're going to do everything we can, whether we have the money or not."

How does the Cabrillo Community College MESA program work at the pre-college level?

"My students at Cabrillo help mentor the Saturday Academy, some of the high school MESA kids help at the junior high, and some of the junior high kids visit elementary schools to talk to the students about science."

With this self-help approach, Hart may just be successful. "The name 'community college' is appropriate, and I think it is time for MESA to be part of that community," he says.

Betty McTier and Robin Williams: Bolstering the Junior MESA Program

"My first involvement with MESA was at Centennial High," says teacher Betty McTier. "The assistant principal asked me to take over the program. At that time it was not doing too well. We started with about ten active members and over a period of five years it had grown to about seventy-five members.

"Long Beach Center Director Julian Zaragoza, before he moved to State-wide, served as my mentor. The center director has a lot to do with the success of the program. It's just like in sports—you're only as strong as your coach. The center directors serve as the leaders and the program will only be as strong as they are. However, in the case of a mature program with experienced personnel, the program survives even with a weak center director. The down side is, however, that in this circumstance there are a number of things we couldn't participate in, such as field trips, because of lack of money."

McTier had been a high school MESA advisor for twelve years but in 1992 took on a Compton, California middle school. "I currently teach seventh grade math. I have taught physics, chemistry and biology."

She offered her views at the PG&E-sponsored MESA Advisors Institute in San Ramon, California. "This is the fourth time I have attended and it just gets better and better. I've been able to go back and use a lot of the ideas and things presented here."

McTier anticipates the challenge of starting up a new middle school program. With her high school experience she feels that it will be a success. "One of the reasons for the successes of the many students I taught in high school was because of MESA. Those students who have been in the program at the middle school level have an edge on their high school classmates. They know practically everything about it and they are looking forward to the type of activities the program provides.

"MESA is particularly important in the Compton area, which is 'inner city,' the population being largely Hispanics and African-Americans. If we didn't have MESA, a lot of these students would never set foot on a college campus. And, in fact, many of them would probably never even get outside of Compton. My plea to all of the sponsors of the MESA program is, 'Please don't stop your contributions because we do need you.'"

Robin Williams, in her tenth year as MESA advisor at Binatta Middle School, got involved at the onset of Junior MESA. Compton was one of the pilot programs. "Each year we have about fifty students in the program coming from the sixth through eighth grades," she says. "When our leadership is real good at the MESA center, our program flows real well. When it is not, the program falls behind. University support provided by the center director is important because it makes MESA students really interested and they want to get involved in the many things we are able to do. I meet with the students twice a week for an hour after school. That really keeps them motivated and involved and they always know what's going on."

How do other kids view MESA?

"They want to get into the program when they see the activities we are involved in. They think the things we do are exciting and they would like to join. Unfortunately, I can only handle about fifty students so I cut it off at that level. I could have many more if I could handle it.

"I think MESA is an excellent program overall. I've had students come back to me after they have graduated from high school and gone on to college. They tell me, 'If I hadn't been in the MESA program, I would never have had these opportunities.' More students make it because early on they become familiar with college life, college situations, and I think that's a big boost.

"I've been coming to the MESA Advisors Training Institute for the past four years and I think it's fabulous. We can go right back in September and put everything we learn to use. I hope they will continue it because that's one way we get training as MESA advisors."

Chapter 11
How Others View MESA

"The MESA program is clearly on its way to achieving its major goals and objectives," Cecil Shaw said in a report on the program in 1973, just two-and-a-half years after the program began. "Basic program components and the involvement and commitment of the many persons involved in implementing the MESA program should be continued," added Shaw, who had been retained by the Lawrence Hall of Science as an outside program evaluation consultant to see if MESA was effective.

In the early years, not everyone viewed it in a positive light. In 1973, a letter to the editor of the *Contra Costa Times* from an El Sobrante, California, woman stated,

> ...school districts (as we are now in the Richmond Unified School District) enroll minority students in the MESA program for special tutoring, counseling, field trips, and cash incentive scholarship awards and still feel the need to add a monthly stipend (handout) for the achievers to the tune of $50 a month! (All of which is tax money.)

MESA responded with a letter that thanked her for helping publicize the program and corrected her last two statements—there were no monthly stipends and no tax money was involved.

In 1982 the Hewlett Foundation commissioned the Center for the Study of Evaluation at the University of California, Los Angeles, to evaluate the MESA program. Its report stated:

> The results (of the study) indicate that the MESA program is well-implemented with a coherent, integrated programmatic framework, and a set of

component services in place that reaches targeted students. Further, the MESA program is perceived as effective by coordinators, advisors, parents and students. These perceptions are borne out by data on academic performance indicating that MESA students perform significantly higher than students of the same ethnic background nation-wide and than other college-preparatory students in their own schools. Further, there is some evidence that MESA students are closing the historic gap in performance between ethnic minority students and white students as indicated by similar levels of performance to college-bound seniors of all ethnic backgrounds statewide and nationally (except in the area of verbal skills where the difference still remains). However, when the performance of MESA students planning to pursue math-based fields is compared nationally (regardless of ethnic background), there are some indications that MESA students may be somewhat less well prepared than the students with whom they will be required to compete.

In response to that last finding, the MESA Minority Engineering Program was initiated to assure that MESA students could compete with other students at the university level. The junior MESA program began somewhat later, also based on the recommendation of the UCLA report.

In its reports the California Postsecondary Education Commission viewed MESA's accomplishments with favor and recommended continued funding and some expansion (see Chapter 10). These reports pointed out program weaknesses and, for the most part, MESA took appropriate steps.

A different report, published in the *Carnegie Quarterly* (reprinted with permission from Vol. XXXV/Nos. 3, 4 Summer/Fall 1990), takes one right into the classroom with MESA study sessions in progress, as the following excerpts reveal. This story by Avery Russell was so much in demand that, for the first time in its history, the *Quarterly* reprinted the edition. The full article follows:

Ensuring Minorities' Success in Mathematics, Engineering, and Science: The MESA Program

Forty students in a college-of-engineering classroom in Berkeley are discussing the base2 logarithm table. They fall into lively debate over whether 2E0 should equal zero, one, or blank. While arguing the pros and cons of this, they review the system of logarithms, the additive law for the multiplication of exponential terms, and the law of exponents for division.

Their teacher asks whether they think it is easier to read down the base2 logarithm table or up the table: "Do you want to explain, Azziza?"

"I think it's easier to go down because you learned it going down."

"And what do you do to get the next entry as you go down?"

"You add it together...I mean you multiply the number times itself."

"Okay," the teacher nods, addressing the room. "And do you remember what that's called? It's called the Principle of the —"

"Preceding Problem!" a voice pipes up.

"Yes. You use the problem before to get the next problem, right? Now. Who can explain why they think it's easier to go up the quadrant of the table? Do you have an idea, Gloria?"

Gloria struggles. "You just, like...if 2E is 32, you subtract...like divide it by 2 and, um, like it's 16, so 2E4 would be 16."

"Okay. So let's try going up a bit. Using what you just said, 2E3 would be—"

"Eight," says the class.

"And what does the E stand for?"

"Exponentiation!" the students explode.

"Good. And 2 exponentiation 2 equals . . .4, 2E1 equals 2, and 2E0 equals 1." The teacher glances around. "I see disagreement. Now who's showing zero? Okay. I see a couple of zeros. Eduardo, can you explain the zero?"

"Well, the 2E0 means take 2 and write it zero times." He reasons, "There's no possible way to get to 1 when you say take 2 and write it zero times."

"Okay," the teacher says hesitantly. "So it sounds like zero. You have Rosy agreeing with you. Dario's agreeing, but Jasmine is disagreeing. Quite a few people are convinced by what you just said. Jasmine, why are you disagreeing?"

"Because every time you go down, it doubles."

Other students develop Jasmine's point. Eventually, through the constant interplay of question and response, the class comes to understand why 2E0 must equal one rather than zero. From there the students move into a discussion of negative exponents. After they have expanded the logarithm table into this area, they work through a series of problems requiring them to add negative exponents. At last they come to fractions. This in turn leads them to discuss another problem raised by the teacher—the sum of an infinite series—which requires that they learn how to add fractions.

Until now, none of the students has known how to add or multiply fractions, and they normally would resist learning this. Presented in the context of some interesting mathematics, however, the arithmetical skills are quickly mastered. The students have come a long way from the base2 logarithm table of the previous hour.

The **individuals** in the classroom are not first-year college freshmen or even high school seniors; they are fourth, fifth, and sixth graders from inner-city schools in Berkeley, East Oakland, and Richmond, where some of the poorest and academically lowest-achieving children in the area live. The children are participating voluntarily in a four-hour-long Saturday Academy of the University of California at Berkeley's precollege Mathematics, Engineering, Science Achievement, or MESA, program, which has an overall enrollment of 600 students from East Bay Area schools. In two hours the students have had only one break to go to the bathroom and fortify themselves with a snack. Otherwise they remain rooted to their seats, their eyes fixed on the teacher and the blackboard, their minds fully engaged in the battle with higher mathematical problems.

The person standing before them is Jane Molnar, a visiting teacher of mathematics in different Bay Area schools. She and five other teachers have been recruited to the faculty of the Saturday Academy by the resourceful Victor Cary, director of Berkeley's precollege MESA center. For four hours each Saturday over a nine-week semester, they subject their enthusiastic charges—240 fourth through twelfth graders—to intensive integrated study of English, mathematics, and science. "They have total academic freedom," says Cary. "We want to release the creativity of the teachers." The instructors work under a broad mandate to promote problem solving, an understanding of concepts, cooperative learning, and "functional transfer skills"—emphasizing the practical and applied. Cary adds, "These intellectual tools are fun to use. The aim is to have fun with this, so students can see how to have a good time with the disciplines."

Molnar brings to the MESA academy a deep love of both children and mathematics as well as teaching experience steeped in the "group discovery method" developed by the late mathematician William Johntz. As his disciple, she has taken the Socratic oath: she has sworn to teach through the art of asking questions, seducing students away from their passive role as rote learners. Asking them questions elicits a steady stream of responses that enables Molnar at each moment to gauge their level of understanding and to create the next question. As she inquires and, if needed, subtly clarifies, the children answer, debate, refute, insist, and ask questions of their own. Their expressions are alert, shifting through joy, frustration, intense concentration, puzzlement, laughter, skepticism, and conviction.

Such success in teaching mathematics to youngsters often typed by their regular teachers and by standardized tests as "slow" is based not only on the Socratic-style group-discovery format but on Molnar's obvious respect for the children and their abilities.

"The philosophy that all children, and not just a select few, are highly talented and capable if taught in the right way, could be used by any teacher with children from any background," she asserts. "The brains of the kids are not the problem. The problem is never the kids' brains."

Getting Minority Kids on the College Track

The idea that children from disadvantaged backgrounds will rise, when challenged and supported, to undreamed heights of intellectual accomplishment underlies MESA's own approach to instruction and learning. It is an expectation that MESA staff members and teacher/advisors constantly reinforce as they provide their students the counseling, study skills, tutoring, and other incentives to get on—and stay on—the college track to scientific and technical careers.

MESA was founded twenty years ago as a school-based academic support program "to increase the number of historically underrepresented students who graduate from four-year universities with a degree in engineering, computer science, or other math-based fields." Its specific aim is to ensure that California's growing population of ethnic minority youth completes four years of college preparatory mathematics and English in addition to chemistry and physics—a tall order for those who may be the first in their families to contemplate going to college and whose parents often have not been formally educated beyond the sixth or eighth grade.

Begun in 1970 with only twenty-five pupils at Oakland Technical High School, the MESA precollege program has since served more than 35,000 young people throughout the state from the fourth grade through high school. More than 10,000 are enrolled for the 1990-91 academic year, a majority of them African American and Mexican American, with a small percentage Puerto Rican and Native American. More than half are girls.

In 1993, with statewide headquarters at Berkeley's Lawrence Hall of Science, precollege MESA operated under a decentralized structure of four regional directors, who guided twenty MESA centers based at University of California and California State University campuses (California Polytechnic State University at San Luis Obispo; California State University at Bakersfield, Chico, Fresno, Fullerton, Long Beach, Los Angeles, and Northridge; Capitol Cities—CSU Sacramento, UC Davis, Santa Rosa Satellite; Central Region Cabrillo Community College; Mid-Peninsula—Foothill Community College, San Francisco State University; Harvey Mudd College; Loyola Marymount University; San Diego State University; San Francisco State University; San Jose State University; University of California at Berkeley and at Santa Barbara; University of the Pacific; and University of Southern California; and at a few other private institutions besides.) These centers currently administer MESA programs in 240 schools spread over seventy school districts. Additionally, more than 3,500 undergraduates in twenty colleges and universities sponsor the allied MESA Engineering Program (MEP), a support system for undergraduates that was established by statewide MESA in 1983 as another link in its educational continuum.

Recognizing the need to intervene earlier if more students were to meet the prealgebra and pregeometry requirements for joining MESA, the program launched Junior MESA in the mid-1980s, incorporating middle and junior high schools that funnel students into high schools offering the program. Two-year support toward the expansion and refinement of Junior MESA was given by the Corporation in 1987. That program received an important vote of confidence during 1989 from the California Postsecondary Education Commission (CPEC), the watchdog for the state legislature, which conducted a year-long evaluation and recommended its continued expansion into all such "feeder" schools. The commission noted that the program has had a "significant positive impact" on the students' course selection, career planning, and aspirations for higher education. (*Evaluation of the Junior MESA Program*, a report to the Legislature in response to Assembly Bill 610 [Hughes] of 1985. California Postsecondary Education Commission. October 1989.)

Extension of MESA down to the fourth grade is still being pilot-tested, as is the precollege program inaugurated at Sherman Indian High School in Riverside, administered by the Harvey Mudd College center. An effort already under way is to encourage promising community college students to transfer into engineering departments at four-year institutions at the beginning of their junior year. MESA centers are also trying to bring more MEP and other college students into the precollege programs as tutors, mentors, and role models for younger students.

While MESA's support comes largely from the state, school districts, and private foundations, with sponsoring colleges and universities contributing offices and staff, California's business community has played a crucial role in the organization's life. Having an evident self-interest in broadening the pipeline of minority members coming into the work force well trained in mathematics and science, corporations this year have contributed nearly $2 million in in-kind and monetary support. In addition to providing grants, scholarships, and awards, they loan executives and professionals to the cause and provide summer jobs and internships. The four-way partnership of the private sector with MESA, higher education, and the public schools indeed is the rock on which the program stands.

MESA has thus evolved into a broad-based, comprehensive outreach service that, since 1981, has helped to turn out 7,261 high school graduates and, since 1983, 2,000 engineering graduates. MESA's evaluation data show that nearly 80 percent of MESA's high school students go on to college after graduation, whereas only 57 percent of all California's graduates continue. MESA students' SAT scores are on average 50 to 75 points higher than those of their non-MESA peers. Seventy-three percent of MESA students enroll in four-year institutions, as opposed to 13 percent for the state's disadvantaged minorities as a whole. Furthermore, about 75 percent of MESA's graduates have a 3.0 or better grade point average (GPA), and two-thirds declare a math-based major as freshmen.

Equally impressive, 3,200 engineering and computer science majors were part of the MESA Engineering Program in 1988-89, and the college retention rate for MEP members continues to be about 63.3 percent—equal to that for Asians and higher than that for Anglos. By contrast, the attrition rate among non-MEP Black and Hispanic engineering students in the state is more than 80 percent. MEP graduates go right on to graduate school or into the professions.

The Magic Combination of Challenge and Support

"It is a total support network that includes a partnership with parents," Cary says about MESA. To Frances Powell, principal of Pasadena's Wilson Middle School which carried the program, "MESA gives moral support in a world that is stressful and competitive. It promotes the bonding, the sharing, the trusting that these children need. One of the unique things it offers is the mentoring and role models—and the hands-on instruction. Right now our curriculum is not hands-on. It is not turning kids on to science. So I take what I learn from MESA and apply it back in the classroom."

The level of intervention MESA offers varies according to the school site. As Cary explains, "the districts are in different stages of development, and MESA has to adapt to the needs and resources of the school community." All participating schools have at least one and as many as five advisors (as in the Sacramento area MESA programs).

A MESA advisor is usually a regular math or science teacher who is given released time or a stipend; an advisory team can include a math and science teacher, an English teacher, counselor, and administrator. To Cary, the most successful MESA classes meet daily during the regular school day, but, emphasizes Betty Farris, MESA's assistant director at the Harvey Mudd College center, "an awful lot of work can get done before and after school and during the lunch hour."

As an elective, MESA periods must compete for children's time and commitment with sports, music, and other electives or extracurricular activities— sometimes an after-school job like a paper route that brings in extra family income, "but the program has rarely lost a student," says Farris. Explains Linda Dell'Osso, MESA director at Harvey Mudd College, "One high school kid in MESA—our smartest one—dropped out of school seven weeks before graduation. His parents divorced. He was suddenly going to school ten miles from home. He couldn't handle it. But he's the only MESA kid we've had who has dropped out. Another kid from Pomona High had severe personal problems.

But he stayed in school and in the program because of his involvement with a strong group of MESA students and advisors."

By law "outside" educational interventions like MESA cannot teach the regular curriculum, but that does not hamper MESA advisors—their ideas, taken from the most advanced curricular innovations, are in the vanguard of change. MESA activities stress certain themes that cut across the disciplines, such as measurement and probability, matter and the environment, to demonstrate the real-world applications of math and science. By fostering the growth of analytical, observational, and mathematical skills that reinforce and extend classroom learning, not duplicate it, the program tries to prepare students for the rapidly changing environment in which they must live.

Comments MESA advisor Garrett A. Duncan, a chemistry teacher at Pomona Junior High School, "I work on motivation and critical thinking, and I engage them in hands-on activities like constructing model rockets and bridges that have to work. Once the students become aware that the emphasis is on applied science, I move to prepare them for MESA Day competitions. We've got to stimulate, direct, and energize these kids."

Duncan, whom Betty Farris swears "runs on five cylinders," does just that. "MESA embarrasses the science programs throughout the state," Duncan declares.

MESA Days—regional competitions in science, engineering, math, and English—are held every spring and feature science and engineering demonstrations, competitions in nine categories, and industry career fairs. The whole year is topped off with an awards banquet honoring the achievements of MESA students, many of whom receive college scholarships to recognize their exceptional progress.

James Harold, Capitol Center MESA's director in Sacramento, the largest center with 2,400 students in the program, is convinced that the academic, college, career, and personal counseling that MESA offers is crucial to its staying power. In overburdened schools with high minority enrollments, there can be as few as one counselor to every 600 students. "The result is," says Lois Slavkin, regional director of the Los Angeles Basin MESA programs, "the students don't have the knowledge and information about which courses to take and the need to pursue a curriculum that places them on a college track." Harold, a former counselor himself, goes further: "At some schools our very best efforts can be defeated by counseling. The students are oftentimes funneled back into prealgebra at the ninth grade, even though they took it in the eighth. In these cases they are lucky if MESA gets to them before the counselor does." In his view, "it is important to get some of the students just exposed to the hard courses, because it is so much easier for them to take other courses and make better grades."

He adds, "in order to get students to commit to a career, we work with them over the long haul. We focus their career interests. Most of them at the start don't want to take math and science. But MESA changes their minds."

Guidance requires the capacity for empathy. "We really need to listen to these kids and offer them alternatives, not advice," believes Harold. "They need to be able to feel there is a thinking, reasonable adult who will listen to them."

The six-week summer enrichment programs and Saturday academies offered by some of the centers add as many as forty days of intensive, structured academic work to the 180-day school year. That is enough to make a difference in a student's grade point average and SAT scores. "A kid who enrolls in both the summer school and the Saturday academy is getting a lot of shots at it," maintains Harold. Summer school gives students a head start on the fall, boosting confidence and cementing the gains of the previous year. Cary agrees, "Some miraculous things can happen during the summer."

To open students to a wide variety of career alternatives in engineering and science, MESA advisors organize field trips to businesses, plants, museums, botanical gardens, space centers, and other "science-rich" institutions in the community. Guest speakers from these resources are invited to class to impart valuable information and serve as role models. Often these MESA "presentations" are made by MESA and MEP graduates currently in the professional workplace.

Teacher preparation is a big concern. To train MESA advisors in high-quality, up-to-date, field-tested curricula and teaching methods compatible with the new science, math, and English frameworks being issued by the California Department of Education, MESA organizes periodic teacher training conferences. The new ideas and tools that advisors bring back to MESA students infuse regular classroom instruction as well, and the whole school benefits.

Parents and "significant other" adults are an essential part of the support network. Without their involvement, many youngsters would not persevere in the program. Comments Harold, "Parents often try to protect their children from the risks of aspiration to higher things. They want to protect them from failure." MESA tries to overcome that well-meant protectiveness by making families partners in their children's school experience. "Many parents have had terrible experiences with schools," observes Betty Farris. "Some teachers will not let a parent inside their doors." Through MESA, parents learn to be advocates for their children's education. One of the best organized parent groups is in Berkeley, but at all centers parents are reached and brought into the program by MESA staff. "Four of my children in college right now are MESA graduates," says one parent. "One of my sons is at Davis (University of California). They all have MESA to thank for their push and enthusiasm."

Students enjoy the strong bonds they form with their MESA peers. They work, play, and study together, compete with other MESA teams on MESA Days, and come to the rescue with a pep talk when one of the group becomes discouraged. Many adolescents are acutely afraid of being typed as a "nerd" if they do well in their studies. Girls may pay an especially heavy social penalty for being smart. Explains Yvonne, a student at John F. Kennedy High School in Sacramento, "You're not supposed to be smart. The big thing is looking good, dressing in the latest fashion, being attractive. MESA," she says, "teaches you that it's okay to be a good student. It teaches that it's okay to be smart in English, math, and science."

"Another thing," says Harold. "There can be in-fighting among underrepresented groups. Often it is not all right to talk to a person of another race. MESA provides brotherhood."

"MESA students are looked up to because they are known for being good at what they do," believes Garrett Duncan. "They're their own free thinkers. That's what I like about the program"

Focus on the Average Student

MESA programs do not exclude mathematically minded students but recruit minority members essentially from the middle range of academic achievement. "We won't take only kids who will make it without us," says Jim Harold.

Berkeley's Cary adds, "I ask counselors to identify promising students who have that shine in their eyes. I do look at their CTBS (California Test of Basic Skills) scores and their grade point averages. And I interview the kids. But I don't rely on scores. If I did I would miss a lot of talented kids."

The need to nurture all available talent indeed is one of the primary rationales for MESA: Employers will not obtain an adequate supply of well-educated personnel by skimming only the most gifted, as determined by standardized tests. That "luxury" has gone with the decline in the size of the youth cohort.

The big stars in their schools, in any event, do not always fare well in college, staff of the MESA engineering programs have discovered. "Giftedness as measured by high GPA and test scores is not a predictor of success," says Madeleine Fish, director of the MESA Engineering Program at California State University, Sacramento. "It is the brightest who are often at the greatest risk. Many of them are academic loners."

Agrees Cary, "They are not prepared for what they will confront in college. MEP students who went through MESA have had their study skills honed. And they have benefited from the group interaction and cooperation that precollege MESA fosters and MEP continues."

Tony Gutierrez, workshop supervisor in Berkeley's MEP, adds: "During their freshman and sophomore years, the stars are more likely to goof off. By the time junior year rolls around, when the amount of work doubles, their study habits have gone to pot."

"Average students," Cary notes, "are used to working their butts off. The work ethic is more defined for them."

Gutierrez cites himself as an example. He entered Berkeley in 1981 as an engineering student. "We didn't have college prep at our school in Oakland, but my older brother was interested in math and I was influenced by him." Gutierrez joined MEP, taking full advantage of its workshops and other supportive services. "I was used to working hard and not having an extensive social life," he says. "I was very disciplined then." During the summers he worked in industry and then, upon graduation, at Los Alamos National Laboratory. After getting his master's degree in solid state physics, he decided that a research and development career was not what he wanted. "I took a position at the patent office in Washington, D.C., and I found administration. I realized I wanted to work more with people." Now that he leads an MEP workshop himself, he is doing for others what his own MEP workshop leader, Antoinette Torres, did for him. "The more I give," he says, "the more I receive."

Gutierrez deplores the attitude in industry that low grade point averages are not acceptable. "Certain firms will only interview students with a high grade point cutoff. But that often ignores the merit and quality of the person."

Jaime White, the coordinator of Project Success, a new initiative of MEP, seems to agree. "Not all those with a 3.0 or 3.5 grade point average are going to be successful. A Hewlett-Packard Company engineer did a correlational analysis betwen high GPAs and career success among its engineers. There was zero correlation. The message is, 'Don't always go out for the student with the highest GPA.'"

The MESA program is demonstrating that many minority children considered of less than stellar ability in math and science can, when challenged and supported, perform well in these disciplines. "Expectations of minority youngsters' performance are generally far, far too low in today's schools," believes Cary. "If you don't demand that students excel, they won't." As Gutierrez puts it, "You give kids a reason not to learn, they'll take it." The converse is equally true, which MESA is proving. Says Cary, "We have only one standard, and that's excellence."

Integration and Diffusion

MESA's statewide office recently received a large grant from the California Postsecondary Education Commission, which will enable Capitol Center's MESA to extend the program down to kindergarten. It will also permit further training of teachers in MESA elementary and junior high schools.

Even so, MESA at present is able to reach only about 4 percent of the target ethnic groups. Acknowledges Cary, "We're very efficient, but all we are able to do is continue the trickle. We can't open the floodgates."

Can the MESA model be assimilated into the larger school context? To Cary, "it could if certain things were in place." With the infusion of new money, MESA could penetrate more schools. MESA director James Harold has made Capitol Center the largest of the MESA centers by persuading school districts to "buy in" to the program. "Two-thirds of our MESA program is cash funded by the districts," he says. "We do have the financial base to start up programs elsewhere." With little additional state support coming through headquarters at the Lawrence Hall of Science, the only significant new money, then, may have to come from the school districts. "We could double the population of MESA students if we had more district buy-ins throughout the state," maintains Harold.

Partnership with the districts not only assures extra funding for expansion, it increases MESA's chances of becoming institutionalized in the schools. MESA cannot succeed without the commitment of school administrators and teachers, which it has achieved despite some initial skepticism about the value of the program and ongoing concern among non-MESA parents and students over the exclusion from full membership of students from groups considered fully represented in math- and science-based fields. (They may participate as associate members in activities such as study periods.) "MESA does benefit the entire student body," says Harold. "This may be one reason why there is so little antagonism. This is a service needed for all students. I tell administrators, parents, and industry people they should be working on the state legislature to get those services for all."

One of the aims under the CPEC grant, according to Carol Fields, administrative analyst at the statewide office, "is to see whether we can induce a MESA-like atmosphere in the whole school, thereby affecting more underrepresented students." Both administrators and MESA staff see the program as a laboratory that, in Cary's words, "tests out curricular ideas and teaching methods that eventually can be adopted schoolwide." Cary is one who believes that "what is good for MESA is good for the schools." In sum, says Harold, "When you introduce MESA, you introduce changes that improve the curriculum for all."

"If I were principal," muses Cary, "I would totally reorganize the schools, and I would implement the MESA program. In my dream I would mainstream all remedial students back into the regular classroom, then organize the school population into smaller units. You can't have a big homogeneous population in the schools.

"But," acknowledges Cary, "I don't think the school structure as it now is can accommodate MESA. We have it backwards. In graduate school you have a small student-teacher ratio. In elementary school you have a class of thirty, and teachers are expected to do everything and deal with a spectrum of children from gifted to remedial. At junior high school, there are five classes a day of forty minutes each. Teachers don't have time enough to prepare adequately. It's just physically impossible. I don't think classes should be held every day. Students should have a good block of time for study and teachers for followup and review. There should be a one-and-a-half to two-hour tutorial for each student to reinforce the lesson and to do homework."

It may be years before the MESA model becomes conventional school practice, but as an academic support program and a bridge between the systems—universities, industry, and the schools—it has inspired similar efforts in at least seven other states: Arizona, Colorado, South Dakota, New Mexico, Oregon, Washington, and North Carolina. Vinetta Jones, former director of the MESA-like Mathematics & Science Education Network in North Carolina, was originally on MESA statewide's staff at the University of California's Lawrence Hall of Science. The College of Engineering, University of Colorado at Denver, is very closely modeled on the California version. Starting in 1980 with thirty young people as members, it now has more than 2,000 students in seventy-nine schools, of whom 44 percent are Hispanic and 54 percent are girls.

Clearly, for MESA to succeed, the schools themselves, as Harold puts it, "have to own the program." And they do. "While the school people may groan about another program being imposed upon them from outside, MESA avoids this image." MESA, in fact, is not just a program, it is a vision of what education should be.

Students in a MESA program at Valencia Park Elementary School

Chapter 12
What the Future Holds

At an early year-end banquet in Berkeley, Bill Somerton, co-founder of MESA, recalls saying, "'I'm looking forward to the day when we don't have a MESA program; don't need a MESA program.' That statement shocked the people. I think they were about to run me off when it dawned on them what I was saying. The ultimate goal is to bring the whole educational system up to a point where MESA is no longer needed."

In contrast, Christina Frausto, a MESA advisor at Southerndale Middle School in San Jose, says, "I just hope MESA is here for as long as mankind is in existence. It's going to help our children decide what their future can be."

"If we can't get our kids through school, we can't get them into the work force," says Rudy Murrieta, a consultant to former California Assemblyman Chacon. A final decision on the form of this expansion was slated for the fall of 1992.

Assemblyman Tom Bates, at the 20th anniversary celebration for MESA, said he's looking forward to the day when there are 80,000 students in the MESA pre-college program, which would be a ten-fold increase over the 1990 level.

"I think," says Bruce Hamlett, "the strategies that make MESA successful are generic kinds of things that could be applied to all students generally in various other kinds of career areas at the 7-12 grade level and the collegiate level as well. Ideally, the best way is to not have a MESA program but to give each school and student the benefits of the kinds of services MESA provides." Hamlett served as an associate director of the California Postsecondary Education Commission and now heads the New Mexico Commission on Higher Education.

Fred Easter, executive director of Statewide MESA, sees inclusion of the community colleges into the MESA network as the most important expansion need for 1993 and beyond. The MESA Minority Engineering Program support services should be introduced into other math-based disciplines at the university level as well as at community colleges, he says. The potential of this type expansion will need watching, he adds.

The foregoing comments reveal the need for MESA and presuppose two expectations:

First, MESA as it now exists continues serving students and producing the results expected by its backers, volunteers and student participants. As MESA approaches its 25th anniversary, it must guard against the tendency to take its model and operations for granted, says Robert Finnell, executive director from 1977 to 1983. MESA expanded in 1977 and obtained private and public support a few years later because it focused on results, not on the number of students served.

What does it take to produce more secondary school graduates with the option of choosing a math-based field of study at the university level?

"Careful delivery of services to students by a trained team of professionals and volunteers," he says, "careful record keeping and reporting, and measuring the influence of the MESA services on the increased number of students graduating with MESA requirements, then matriculating at a college or university."

The same held true for MESA's role in the 1980s in the university level effort in engineering schools and in junior high, community college and elementary school programs. Unlike entitlement and other mandated programs supported by state funds, MESA never enjoyed the luxury of automatic financial support. As it expands and sustains its programs, MESA must continue showing that it makes a positive difference in the number of underrepresented minority students who graduate from universities and colleges in math-based fields, he maintains.

The second expectation relates to various paths educational institutions take in the future. "Certainly if our public and private high schools are staffed, funded and organized to produce an appropriate share of prepared graduates from MESA's target population, then the MESA program would be redundant," Finnell says. "Should this occur, educators and former students will toast MESA and remember its striving for that goal in difficult economic and social times. Presumably one final celebration would occur and MESA would retire. As we write in early 1993, that scenario becomes increasingly unlikely."

On the other hand, California Assembly Bill 3237 calls for phased expansion of MESA in all secondary schools with 40 percent enrollment of low income and underrepresented minority students. But tenuous state finances and difficulties at the local level make it unlikely that a timely expansion could occur. Perhaps a third alternative will become the scenario for MESA's future in California and other states.

Given the present condition of local and state educational budgets and the need for MESA's program in a large number of secondary schools, the most likely case for the program's expansion is on a school district by school district level. Since a local district could fund its own MESA program for about a 6 percent add-on to an existing school budget, a district could allocate its scarce funds to a MESA start-up and annually renew the funding as the program takes hold.

The current climate bodes well for this option and suggests that it is

Sailcar race at a MESA Day in Sacramento   —Photo by John Jernegan

the most likely. National, regional, and local pressures are mounting to improve the quality and output of elementary and secondary schools so our work force can compete in a complex, technologically oriented, global economy where rival nations give high priority to preparing their youth for a competitive environment. As American industry continues its restructuring, and the country reallocates its military funding to peace time efforts following the end of our competition with the former Soviet Union, parallel shifts could occur in terms of restructuring public and private education and focusing on the level of academic preparation achieved by high school graduates.

Thus, local school districts could choose to include a MESA initiative in its mix of reforms and programs. The availability of a model with a clear objective and set of educational approaches, a set of tools for orienting and training staff and volunteers, and a record of more than two decades of achievement could result in a step by step expansion of MESA. And since this scenario responds to local demand, it could well be a matter of making a virtue of necessity, Finnell believes.

MESA evolved from the identification of a particular need and a specific educational opportunity that existed at a high school in the late 1960s. In its early years students, teachers, principals, parents and corporate volunteers discussed ways of meeting the need: preparing underrepresented minority students for math-based fields of study. They proposed solutions, modified them, discarded others, and tested the model. As the program expanded, a model was defined and in the mid-1970s expanded as a result of major investments by the Sloan and Hewlett foundations. And a further expansion, made possible in the late 1970s and early 1980s by California funding, brought additional growth of both the secondary and postsecondary level. So the MESA expansion has come from the grass roots and the top down.

In the 1990s we are seeing a demand for our institutional leaders to listen to what the average citizen recognizes as a need. Whether it is how our local schools organize or define goals, American citizens can set the agenda. A MESA model at a school or home where adults teach, then, is a choice that can be encouraged and made without waiting for authority figures or decisions from "on high."

Nothing in the MESA model is esoteric, complex, or attainable only by an initiated few. It is a model achievable within a home, a neighborhood, or a school. It aims at developing the talent youth possess and tapping that energy for the total society. The decision to move could come from a high school student, a parent, a teacher, or a concerned citizen. Particularly in today's world it is a positive creative response to channeling our youth into productive lives.

Fred Easter:
Keeping the Steeds in Harness

When Fred Easter interviewed for the position as executive director of MESA, it was the first time he had been west of Minnesota. He joined the program in June 1986.

"I came to MESA knowing little about it and found it a thankless task because everybody knew more about it than I did," Easter says with a smile. "When you are new and the head of an organization of this size and complexity, everyone assumes you are smart and well-placed in the position. It seemed hopeless the first two years, but now I feel I have my arms around it.

"An interesting and sometimes frustrating part of this job is that everyone in the organization feels the program is **theirs**. High school principals talk about **their** MESA program. Deans talk about **their** MESA program. Even state legislators, Teresa Hughes and John Vasconcellos, talk about **their**

Fred Easter with Wilbur H. Somerton Award recipient Vonna Hammershmit

MESA program. And indeed, each of these people, along with people in the field who also have pride in ownership of the program, plays an important part.

"To run MESA is to have eight Arabian steeds, each tied to one of your fingers by twine," Easter says in reminiscing about his early years. "Directing this program is a challenge. There's no other way to put it. It's impossible. It's also tremendous fun. The people in the organization are extremely dedicated. They really make what happens happen in terms of changes in kids' lives. When you see the actual results of what goes on at a MESA Day or at a science fair in which MESA students compete, you know it's all worth while. But having administrative responsibility for the program is horrendous."

Fred Easter's survival capabilities saw him through the first frustrating years. He's well on his way in solving the myriad problems facing a program of this magnitude. Foremost among these is the program's financial deficit he inherited. When Robert Finnell left as executive director in 1983, the program's reserve fund totaled half a million dollars for emergencies and dealing with late payments of promised financial support. Due to an over-ambitious expansion program and a let-down in the financial development program in the 1983-86 period, Easter inherited a three-quarter-million-dollar deficit.

"In the first three years, I shrank the deficit down to $617,000," Easter says. With an annual total budget of $3.7 million in 1992, and the impact of a recession and state budget woes, small deficits are again occurring.

"With continuing expansion of the program, it will take five to seven years before we are on top of this problem," Easter says. "I hope to build a surplus so, when I retire, I can leave it in the shape that Bob Finnell left it in, but a significantly larger program in terms of the number of students served."

Easter left a position as manager of a Miami division of computer-based educational programs for Control Data Corporation to join MESA. He previously managed a CDC center in New York City.

He was born in Harlem Hospital in New York City.

"I went through the public school system in New York City, skipping two years—third and eighth grades—so when I graduated from high school, I had just turned sixteen a month earlier," Easter says. "I finished in the top half of my senior class and was successful politically. I was vice president and then president of the student government, and I represented the New York City schools at a national conference of student councils in Toledo, Ohio. When I had my appointment with the college counselor, he looked at me and at my record and said, 'You are not college material. Get a job. Next.' Although my parents had one high school diploma between them, my father was very disturbed by this 'counseling.' Some tournament bridge playing friends of my parents recommended I attend a prep school to make up the two years I had skipped. I was the first black student to attend the Gunnery School in Washington, Connecticut, where I received an extraordinarily strong educational back-

ground. Although I played on several athletic teams, I did well enough to receive a scholarship to Harvard. It was a struggle but I did graduate in five years.

"My first job out of college was with Time, Inc., but I decided New York City
was really not a life support system so I accepted a teaching and coaching position in a prep school in Massachusetts. Then after Martin Luther King, Jr., was
assassinated, I was offered a position at Carleton College in Minnesota. There I
became associate director of admissions, associate dean of students, director
of minority affairs and director of the ABC (A Better Chance) program. ABC is a
program that puts students not likely to go to college because of their existing
surroundings into public or private school situations. A high percentage of
these students go on to college. I began working on my doctorate in educational psychology at University of Minnesota, but inflation drove me back into
the job market. That's when I joined Control Data Corporation."

Clearly infected with "MESA fever," Easter says, "I tell people what MESA is
perhaps fifty times a year. What people want to know is, what do you do? How
do you do it? That's all I talk about. I can recite it in my sleep. I can do it with
handouts, without handouts. I can do it in fifteen minutes, I can do it in two
hours. I have one song, and I go sing it. That's all."

Perhaps as important, he knows what MESA is not. "I've never been in the
presence of anyone preaching to kids against drugs or pregnancy as a part of a
MESA activity. We're obviously anti-drugs and anti-teenage pregnancy, but
there's no part of the intervention that teaches safe sex or attempts to make
sure kids know the dangers of drugs. We're basically about math and science
and engineering, and that's what we're feeding the kids. And they respond. If
there is a problem, it is a well-kept secret."

What about MESA's future? "I think the major initiative, and it's already begun, is MESA's move into the community college segment. We will increase
the number of students who graduate with degrees in engineering in the shortest possible time."

Community colleges are more tolerant of students with weaknesses in
their high school backgrounds than four-year institutions and provide capable
students with a second chance, he notes. In a way, community colleges serve
as a filtering mechanism through which deserving and capable students can
enter technical fields of study at four-year institutions. Perhaps because of this,
evidence indicates community college transfer students do as well and, in
some cases, better than students who enter four-year institutions at the freshman level. Easter believes this will add significantly to the number of students
graduating with training in technical fields.

He's also concerned about school kids out there who will never benefit
from a MESA program.

"I see kids who have died and just haven't fallen down," he says. "What's
going to happen to them, and when? Somebody's got to touch them too."

Chapter 13
Applying MESA Principles

MESA cannot claim any magic formula. Most of its principles have been known for a long time and used in other places. MESA uses the collective experiences of many people who care enough about children to invest time and expertise in their future.

To the question of the adaptability of MESA principles for other schools and disciplines, without hesitation, Dr. Joseph Watson responds, "Yes, most definitely it can be adapted. In fact we have used it virtually across the board here at the University of California at San Diego.

"We have a McNeer Grant to increase student participation in science and engineering," says Watson, vice chancellor for Student Affairs. "We use the group study approach, which meets what appears to be a generic problem—students studying in isolation, not having a major immersion in the subject, and lacking exchanges with other students. The MESA approach of students reasoning their way through problems and discussing them with others is a general approach, not something unique to a particular locale or subject matter."

Watson earned his BS degree from City College of New York and his doctoral degree in chemistry from University of California at Los Angeles. He joined the faculty of UC San Diego in 1966 and rose to the rank of professor. After serving as provost of Third College for eleven years, he was appointed vice chancellor of the university in 1981. In this, and his previous post, he has been involved in education administration, including undergraduate enrollment and retention. He has served on many commissions and task forces dealing with academic preparation and undergraduate education.

Watson states, "As MESA has shown, parents must become aware of a school's academic program and become involved in it. Students must be encouraged to discuss academic matters and things of an intellectual nature in a family setting with their parents and siblings. Students should be encouraged along these same lines with their peer groups.

"One important feature of MESA is documenting the outcomes—measuring the differences between pre- and post-performance," Watson says. "Many of the other programs do not have the focus on superior performance as MESA does, being satisfied with retention rather than high academic achievement. MESA has set high goals and objectives that other programs— affirmative action programs—should emulate."

Joseph Watson

Dr. Eugene Cota-Robles views the successful replication of the MESA program from a different perspective. "One reason for MESA's success in engineering is because of the cohesiveness of the engineering profession," he says. "There is a general lack of cohesiveness in other fields, such as physics and chemistry, and this is certainly also true in the liberal arts. The medical field is perhaps an exception in which a MESA-type program would work because, like engineering, medical schools have a commitment, a responsibility, and a cohesiveness we don't see in many other academic fields."

A native-born Mexican-American, Cota-Robles earned his doctorate in bacteriology at the UC Davis. He has served as chancellor of the UC Santa Cruz Crown College and has been a consultant in science education to the National Science Foundation. He also served with the president's office of the University of California. His ties with MESA include chairing its board of directors in the years he served in that body.

"Although MESA works well with some teachers and a selected group of underrepresented minority students interested in science-based fields, in my opinion, its impact on the school system as a whole has been minimal," he says. "My perspective is, if we are really going to make a difference on the larger problem, we're going to have to change the school. People have lost confidence in our schools and that's why voucher systems are being proposed.

"People have the view, with programs that work, you should be able to transport them entirely. But I don't think that's the case. To make them work, it is probably necessary to take in people from the outside and expand from the inside out, as opposed to replication. For example, in engineering, where the program works so well, faculty from math, physics and chemistry should be drawn into the program. The most important thing that happens is the faculty members begin to see that minority students can succeed. They come in with the belief that minority kids can't succeed; they have no confidence in them and no expectations of them. Once they see them up

Eugene H. Cota-Robles

close, such as in advanced courses, it has an impact on the faculty and their attitudes change. The kids begin asking questions; they come in asking for advice and they establish a meaningful relationship with the formerly disbelieving faculty member. This is how MESA can expand into other disciplines.

"A fundamental problem is that low-income and minority families are unable or don't know how to become involved in the education process. In my own case, the high expectations of my family and the support and encouragement they gave me led me to succeed. I am working on a program now at the Lawrence Hall of Science called *Mattmata Familia*—Family Math for Science. The parents of children at the second and third grade levels become involved with the idea of developing family support for their children.

"The inner city is a special problem that needs attention. As part of President Clinton's national service program, young people should be sent into the barrio or the ghetto as part of teaching teams. Here MESA principles could be applied. Someone needs to develop a way of replicating the MESA experience for these people as well as for the teaching community in general.

"Looking toward the future, MESA needs greater visibility. Newspapers don't want things that are not sensational. But perhaps MESA, with the cooperation of industry, could make some television public announcements in which a young black woman or a Latino engineering student is flashed on the screen in the middle of the Saturday morning programming with a brief message—'In MESA, we're the catalyst,' followed by the MESA logo."

Formula for Success

MESA began in 1970 with an emphasis on engineering because of industry's need for qualified graduates in this field. Engineering has long offered upward mobility for minorities and others who lacked history and tradition in professional fields. In scientific and technical fields, where advancement is generally based on technical ability, there is probably less bias.

The same principles governing MESA can probably be applied to other professional fields. The key components of the program include rigorous academic courses for pre-college students with an expectation of academic excellence. Students receive support in the form of tutorials, peer study groups, introduction to role models, and rewards for succeeding. This kind of support requires networking of parents, teachers, school administrators, and industry and business personnel.

A MESA-type program can best be started at the grassroots level. A beginning point might be with parents who want a better education for their children. Education directed towards a professional field is often beyond their hopes but it is achievable with coordinated effort. One parent can't do it alone but a group of parents acting through a PTA or similar organization can develop support for the program. In some cases teachers themselves may initiate a MESA-type program. They may want to begin by contacting parents of students with academic potential and form the essential parent support group in this manner.

MESA-California can provide guidance and strategy to start the program. Interested groups may call MESA-California at 510/987-9337 or write:

> MESA Statewide Office
> University of California
> 300 Lakeside Drive, Seventh Floor
> Oakland, California 94612-3550

A well-organized group of parents with clear goals and objectives can effectively change school policies and practices. Contacts with those teachers who have their students' interests foremost in mind is the next step. Teachers must be informed about the MESA program principles and be drawn into the planning and operation, involved to the point they are convinced it is their program. Ideas can originate and strategies develop in meetings of teachers and parents. They will select a pilot group of interested students who exhibit academic potential. Although past performance is a factor, potential is more important because the MESA program is designed to help each student who participates achieve his or her full potential.

The next step brings in school administrators and people from local businesses and industry. Their approval and support of the program is essential. The school principal, vice-principals, department heads, and school board members must be convinced a MESA-type program will benefit the entire school. One way to accomplish this would be to put them in touch with other school administrations conducting successful MESA programs. MESA-California can provide information on who to contact. Again, as with parents and teachers, school administrators must feel that MESA is their program.

Although MESA-type programs can work at individual schools, it is generally more effective to combine the efforts of a group of schools, preferably within the same school district. Funds may be available on a district-wide basis that would not be available to a single school. When school district officials discover the benefits that accrue to the entire district in improved student performance, they should willingly offer support within their means.

If schools lack sufficient target population to justify a full program, they could band together with neighboring schools using the model developed for the San Juan School District in the Sacramento, California area (see Chapter 10).

College or university officials may help provide leadership for the program if there is an institution of that level near the proposed MESA project. They can contact other colleges or universities that run MESA programs for guidance. Even if an institution is not able to provide formal leadership, informal arrangements can often be made to supply tutors, speakers and role models for the MESA program.

Any program that incorporates MESA services can be successful if it follows the model. But "Getting program leaders to see that there is value in the MESA model, if left alone, can be difficult," says Fred Easter, executive director of MESA-California. "There is a tendency to do the things (in the model) that come easy and not the things that come hard." Organizers should innovate, but Easter predicts the model will fail if the key elements are not retained. Probably the most important of the "hard things" is the demand for academic excellence. Breaks in the network are another potential problem to watch for. All of the support groups are important and failure of any one of them will jeopardize the program.

All students, regardless of ethnicity or grade level, deserve the opportunity to benefit from the type of services that MESA provides. The deterrent to a broad application of the program is the amount of money it would cost. MESA is not an expensive program; for example, an increase in school funding of only 7 percent would make it possible for every student in California to receive MESA services and support. The percentage increase would be even less for most of the other states where per student expenditures for their education are substantially greater than in California. In terms of the resulting increase in the quality of the nation's work force, this investment would produce dividends worth billions of dollars.

Money is important, if just to provide incentive scholarships for students, but it is far from being the only ingredient for running a successful MESA program. People of ability, dedication, and vision are needed to provide program leader-

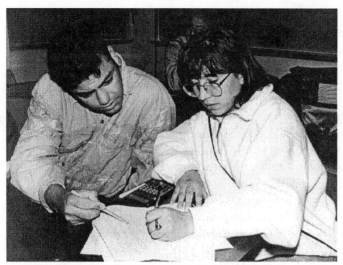

Students at Cal Poly Pomona Academic Excellence Workshop

ship.Volunteers, the backbone of every successful MESA program, serve at every level; in the schools, in the homes of students, and in the community. They also came from local businesses and industrial concerns. No amount of money can buy the services provided by dedicated and knowledgeable volunteers. For example:

Teachers become MESA advisors because they see an opportunity to provide their students services that help them excel in their academic work. These advisors volunteer their time and effort, tutoring and advising students before and after school, during lunch, and on weekend hours. Thomas Ehrlich, president of Indiana University, says it best, "Great teachers have great expectations about what their students can do. But they are careful to let students know what is expected of them. Students, like the rest of us, want to be appreciated, and great teachers show a real interest in their students."

MESA students volunteer their time to advise and tutor their peers, younger students, and students at MESA program feeder schools.

University students and faculty donate their time to host MESA students visiting their campuses. They become mentors and serve as role-models for MESA students. Faculty and staff conduct workshops on study techniques and college application procedures, and act as tutors and resource leaders for study groups. Public school teachers, students, and parents often participate in workshops together.

Industry and business representatives host field trips, serve on advisory boards, act as role-model speakers, tutors, mentors, and supervisors of students on summer jobs. Corporations provide funding, donate equipment for use in classrooms, and provide awards for outstanding achievement by students and teachers. They may also provide summer jobs for students and the use of their facilities for meetings, workshops, and award banquets.

Parents volunteer as role-model speakers, conduct workshops in their areas of expertise for other parents and students, help supervise Saturday Academies, prepare lunches for field trips, and host study groups in their homes.

Both Watson and Cota-Robles point to the importance of parental guidance and support in the education of their children. This subject is so important that the next and last chapter of this book is devoted to how parents can prepare their children for their educational future. That future may involve entry into a MESA program at the secondary school level.

—Photo by John Jernegan

Donnie Gockley, Klem Checo, and Marcus Warner (left to right)
from the Success through Collaboration American Indian program
at Lone Pine display awards won at 1993 Northern California MESA Day

Chapter 14
Preparing Children for MESA

Parental involvement produces the highest level of student achievement. This support and involvement needs to begin long before the student is eligible for the MESA program at the secondary school level. Although in some areas, MESA preparatory programs begin at the elementary school level, this is not a substitute for parental involvement.

Reading, simple concepts of mathematics, and related skills basic to academic success begin at home in a child's early years. Reading to young children can be a satisfying experience for both children and parents. The interest in books this reading stimulates will be a lifelong asset.

Parents should continue reading aloud to their children even as they grow older. An article in the *San Francisco Chronicle* on December 26, 1992, states:

> Many parents stop reading to their children after they reach the age of 8 or 9, and hours of watching television outdistance those spent with books, says a new study released by a teacher's organization. Albert Shanker, president of the American Federation of Teachers, reports, "Clearly there are some things we are not doing right. Kids have to get an idea of the great stuff they are missing (by not reading). They love to be introduced to more adult material. We can't do it without parents."

Researchers found that 52 percent of the parents read daily to their children under eight years of age, but only 13 percent of those with children ages nine to fourteen read to their children every day.

The article points out it is not just a matter of reading aloud to children. "If a parent says, 'Here's my ten minutes of reading to you,' it's not going to work," says Shanker. "Share the things you do as adults."

An article in the *Indianapolis Star* by Peggy Gisler and Marge Eberts, dated November 19, 1993, cites a study by the U.S. Department of Education which finds that one in four students in grades 8 to 12 "never or hardly ever" read for fun. They suggest that parents should make an effort to start focusing their children on reading. The authors suggest eight ways parents can help their children become better readers:

Read yourself. Actions really do speak louder than words. When children see you reading the newspaper or curling up with a book, they'll want to follow your example. Be sure to read books that you really enjoy so your children will observe the pleasure reading brings to you.

Make sure your children read every day. Reading, like shooting baskets or playing the piano, is a skill that improves with practice. Researchers have found that children who spend at least 30 minutes a day reading for fun, no matter what they read, develop the skills to be better readers at school.

Get the library habit. Make sure that each member of your family has a library card. While you're there, check out a book yourself.

Read aloud to your children. Research shows that it is the most important thing parents can do to help their children become better readers. Begin reading to them when they are very young. It is never too early to start.

Keep reading to your children. This exposes older students to more sophisticated sentence structure, vocabulary and organization than they may be comfortable with reading on their own.

Send your children on a scavenger hunt through the newspaper. Have them look for things such as the following: pictures of their favorite athletes, the temperature in a city where a relative lives, three words that begin with "w," and a movie that is playing at a nearby theater.

Give books as gifts. Then find a special place for your children to keep their library.

Make reading a privilege. Say, "You can stay up 15 minutes later tonight if you're reading in bed." Or you might say, "Because you helped with the dishes, I have some time to read you an extra story."

Even if you're not a good reader yourself, you can still encourage your children. As your children learn to read, ask them to read to you. Talk about books your children have read. Ask a friend or relative to read aloud to your children.

A weekly after-school session for second graders

Dr. Tomas Arciniega, president of California State University at Bakersfield (see profile in Chapter 5), credits his advancement to his early interest in reading and the easy access he had to a public library as a child.

Public libraries can be an excellent resource for parents and children. Many libraries offer story-time programs for young children and a variety of programs and reading incentives for older children. Librarians can assist parents and children select books for reading programs at any level. Resources for academic and information needs are available for older students and adults. Students with reading experience from early childhood who know how to use libraries as a resource will be well on their way to success when they reach their "MESA years."

"I was checking my son's homework while a repairman worked in the kitchen," says Evelyn Torres-Rangel, a former MESA school advisor. "He overheard us and his comment was, 'Well, I guess that's what you'd expect from a school teacher.' I was shocked because I assumed that all parents checked their children's homework." The Torres-Rangels take their two boys to museums, serve on the PTA and even shut off the TV set Monday through Thursday. As teachers in a year-round school, they alternated their staying at home with the boys over an eight year span. Their children earn straight A's.

Jim Trelease, author of the best selling *Read Aloud Handbook*, would agree with the Torres-Rangels about the effects of TV on learning ability. In the book he states, "In its short lifetime, television has become the major stumbling block to literacy in America. Television's negative impact on children's reading habits, and therefore their thinking, is enormous."

Trelease recommends a program of controlled TV viewing by children, combined with read-aloud sessions, beginning when the youngsters are infants. The ability to read and a love for reading could be a major step in a child's educational achievement, with or without MESA.

In addition, mathematics is also important in a child's early developmental years. Children can be introduced to the elements of mathematics at an early age. Many activities in a typical day of a preschool child can relate to concepts of mathematics. The approach should always be positive since children, influenced by adult attitudes, often are intimidated by mathematics—afraid of trying to solve problems or victims of the "I hate math" syndrome.

Math, a part of every day life, should be as natural as eating cereal for breakfast. It is more than arithmetic. It relates to the world around us in many ways: How far? How big? How old? How many? Answers to questions like these help describe our world. Other math concepts carry over into science fields: the symmetry of snowflakes, development of the abacus to facilitate arithmetic, techniques of weighing and measuring, computing of quantities in cooking—the list is endless.

Students prepare for a race at
a Northern California MESA Day

—Photo by John Jernegan

In the previous chapter, Cota-Robles mentions his Lawrence Hall of Science program—Family Math for Science—which begins in the second or third grade. The Hall of Science book, *Family Math*, by Jean Stenmark, Virginia Thompson, and Ruth Cossey, outlines a technique for parents and children as young as kindergarten age working together to develop math skills. There are many other fine books and teaching aids on this subject. However, as soon as children learn to talk, an emphasis on numbers will help make math a natural part of their daily lives.

Parents who are knowledgeable about education, in addition to being caring, often provide their children with the sequential experiences that allow children opportunities not only to grow intellectually, but also to learn about the world around them. These parents help their children learn about challenging professions and careers that also match each child's interests and abilities. Once a child is attracted to an area of knowledge, the parents will explore with the child both the rewards and the path to success in that field.

School counselors work with several hundred students at a time so they can only manage to see that students meet the major goals of high school graduation and college entrance requirements. Parents, on the other hand, must deal with the total development of their children. Neither parents nor counselors will necessarily be expert in advising and supporting the math and science interests of their children. This is where a math- and science-based program such as MESA comes in. Professional advice and support in these fields becomes available to students to augment the support of counselors and parents.

If you can imagine the commitment of a family helping a child become a ballerina, a tennis pro or a virtuoso musician, then you can imagine the type of support and nurture students need for careers in math- and science-based fields. Not every child will possess the talent or determination to become world class in his or her field of interest, but each child should have the opportunity to develop fully the talent that is within.

In the following statement by psychologist Haim Ginott, the word "parent" could be substituted for "teacher":

> It is my personal approach that creates the climate. It is my daily mood that makes the weather. As a teacher, I possess tremendous power to make a child's life miserable or joyous. I can be a tool of torture or an instrument of inspiration. I can humiliate or humor, hurt or heal. In all situations, it is my response that decides whether a crisis will be escalated or deescalated, and a child humanized or dehumanized.

MESA is the glue that binds together all of these components—parents, students, and teachers. These, along with the community's resources, can help young people become professionals with rewarding, fulfilling careers. Parents interested in the education of more than their own children can combine their efforts with like-minded citizens. That is what happened when one such group came together in the late 1960s, and as a result, set in motion efforts that became the MESA program.

—Photo by John Jernegan

MESA MEP graduates pose following 1993 ceremony at CSU Sacramento

Appendices

Appendix I
List of the Chairs of MESA Board of Directors*

1977-79 Wilbur H. Somerton, University of California, Berkeley
1979-81 Lee Browne, California Institute of Technology, Pasadena
1981-83 Jaime Oaxaca, Northrop Corporation, Los Angeles
1983-85 Rex Fortune, Superintendent, Inglewood School District
1985-86 Richard Collins, Bechtel Power Corporation, San Francisco
1986-87 Eugene Cota-Robles, University of California, Santa Cruz
1987-88 Richard Pesqueira, Western Regional College Board, Sacramento
1988-91 Lawrence Baack, Pacific Gas and Electric, San Francisco
1991-   Shirley Thornton, California Department of Education, Sacramento

* Source: MESA California

Appendix II
List of Chairs of MESA Industry Advisory Board*

1978-81 Richard Collins, Bechtel Power Corporation, San Francisco
1981-83 Lodwrick Cook, Atlantic Richfield Corporation, Los Angeles
1983-85 Stephen Bryant, Bechtel Power Corporation, San Francisco
1985-86 DuWayne Peterson, Security Pacific Automation, Los Angeles
1986-87 S. Dwight Wheeler, Litton Industries, Woodland Hills
1987-88 David Crain, Southern California Gas Company, Los Angeles
1988-89 Charles Mackdanz, Chevron, USA, San Francisco
1989-90 Rogg Collins, Northrop Corporation, Los Angeles
1990-   Combined functions with MESA Board

*Source: MESA California

Appendix III
List of Companies Providing Financial Support for MESA* **

Activision, Inc.
Aerospace Corporation
Amdahl Corporation
Ampex Corporation
Anheuser-Busch, Inc.
Atari Corporation
Atlantic Richfield Company (ARCO)
AT&T Company
Bank of America
Bechtel Corporation
Bechtel Power Company
Bell Communications Research, Inc.
Bethlehem Steel Corporation
California Casualty Insurance Company
Chevron USA Production Company
CH2M Hill Companies, Ltd.
Convergent Technologies Corporation
Diamond Shamrock, Inc.
Digital Equipment Corporation
Dow Chemical Company
Exxon Corporation
Fluor Corporation
Fluor Daniel, Inc.
Foremost McKesson (FMC)
GenCorp, Inc. - Aerojet Division
General Dynamics Corporation
General Motors Corporation
Geomatrix, Inc.
GTE California Corporation

Hewlett-Packard Company
Hughes Aircraft Company
IBM Corporation
Levine-Fricke, Inc.
Litton Guidance and Control Systems
Lockheed Corporation
Lockheed Missiles & Space Company
Los Angeles Department of Water & Power
Magnavox Electronic Systems Company
McDonnell Douglas Corporation
3M Company
Mobil Corporation
Nissan Design International, Inc.
Northrop Corporation
Occidental Petroleum Corporation
Pacific Gas & Electric Company
Pacific Bell
Printronix, Inc.
Rockwell International Corporation
San Diego Gas and Electric Company
Southern California Edison Company
Southern California Gas Company
Syntex Corporation
Tandem Computers, Inc.
TRW, Inc.
Toshiba America, Inc.
Union Oil Company (Unocal Corporation)
Westinghouse, Inc.
Xerox Corporation

* Contributed $5000 or more
** Source: MESA California

Appendix IV
List of Foundations Providing Financial Support for MESA * **

Ahmanson Foundation
Alcoa Foundation
Allied Signal Foundation
Carnegie Corporation
Joseph Drown Foundation
Foremost-McKesson Foundation
General Electric Foundation
W.R. Hearst Foundation
William and Flora Hewlett Foundation
Hexcel Foundation
Intel Foundation
Walter S. Johnson Foundation
Lockheed Leadership Fund

Medtronic Foundation
Mobil Foundation
NACME Incorporated
National Science Foundation
Pacific Telesis Foundation
Pew Charitable Trusts
Shell Oil Company Foundation
Alfred A. Sloan Foundation
Steelcase Foundation
Mary H. Stuart Foundation
Times Mirror Foundation
Union Oil Foundation
Van Loben Sels Foundation

* Contributed $5000 or more
** Source: MESA California

Appendix V
List of Public Agencies Providing Financial Assistance* **

California Department of Education
California Department of Energy
California Postsecondary Education Commission
National Science Foundation
US Department of Education
US Department of Energy
Public School Districts***
Universities***

* Contributed $5000 or more.
** Source: MESA California.
*** Have contributed substantial funding in support of programs

Appendix VI
Table of Fall Semester Freshman Enrollments in Engineering in the U.S.*

Academic Year	African American	Hispanic American	American Indian	Total Minority	Total Enrollment	Percent Minority
1973-74	1,684	525	40	2,249	51,207	4.4
1974-75	2,447	888	89	3,424	62,582	5.5
1975-76	3,840	1,384	120	5,344	74,558	7.2
1976-77	4,372	1,766	171	6,309	81,652	7.7
1977-78	4,728	2,161	244	7,133	88,256	8.1
1978-79	5,493	2,664	225	8,382	95,171	8.8
1979-80	6,339	3,136	317	9,792	103,090	9.5
1980-81	6,661	3,373	365	10,399	109,314	9.5
1981-82	7,015	3,689	412	11,116	114,201	9.7
1982-83	6,715	3,635	371	10,721	114,517	9.4
1983-84	6,342	3,885	376	10,603	108,763	9.7
1984-85	6,245	3,939	410	10,594	104,374	10.2
1985-86	6,374	3,849	365	10,588	102,285	10.4
1986-87	5,873	3,359	353	9,585	98,298	9.8
1987-88	6,145	3,826	354	10,325	94,814	10.9
1988-89	7,075	4,246	433	11,754	97,379	12.1
1989-90	7,284	4,599	424	12,307	94,791	13.0
1990-91	8,370	5,382	526	14,278	93,705	15.2
1991-92	8,305	5,266	582	14,153	92,308	15.3
1992-93	8,924	5,624	633	15,181	92,699	16.4

*Source: National Action Council for Minorities in Engineering (NACME)

Appendix VII
Table of Fall Semester Undergraduate Enrollments
in Engineering in the U.S.*

Academic Year	African American	Hispanic American	American Indian	Total Minority	Total Enrollment	Percent Minority
1973-74	4,869	2,371	204	7,444	183,520	4.1
1974-75	6,319	3,158	360	9,837	197,899	5.0
1975-76	8,258	3,941	317	12,516	228,183	5.5
1976-77	9,828	5,138	446	15,412	254,797	6.0
1977-78	11,388	5,944	618	17,950	286,500	6.3
1978-79	12,954	7,158	625	20,737	308,556	6.7
1979-80	14,786	8,454	759	23,999	337,807	7.1
1980-81	16,181	9,043	903	26,127	362,300	7.2
1981-82	17,611	10,200	970	28,781	384,162	7.5
1982-83	17,598	10,683	1,078	29,359	400,038	7.3
1983-84	17,817	11,599	1,127	30,543	402,561	7.6
1984-85	17,451	12,202	1,186	30,839	391,052	7.9
1985-86	17,994	12,941	1,120	32,055	379,830	8.4
1986-87	16,830	11,913	1,071	29,814	365,161	8.2
1987-88	17,300	12,981	1,136	31,417	352,848	8.9
1988-89	18,227	13,188	1,164	32,579	342,280	9.5
1989-90	18,939	13,761	1,205	33,905	334,723	10.1
1990-91	20,909	15,917	1,468	38,294	335,102	11.4
1991-92	21,891	16,374	1,538	39,803	335,585	11.9
1992-93	23,136	18,088	1,809	43,033	340,271	12.6

*Source: National Action Council for Minorities in Engineering (NACME)

Appendix VIII
Table of B.S. Degrees Granted to Minority Engineering Students in the U.S. Durring 1970-93*

Year	Total Degrees	African American No.	%	Hispanic American No.	%	American Indian No.	%	Total Minority No.	%
1970	41,069	378	0.92	N/A		N/A		N/A	
1971	41,291	407	0.99	N/A		N/A		N/A	
1972	41,919	579	1.38	N/A		N/A		N/A	
1973	40,950	574	1.40	721	1.76	36	0.09	1,331	3.25
1974	38,574	743	1.93	636	1.65	32	0.80	1,411	3.66
1975	35,217	734	2.08	685	1.95	44	0.12	1,463	4.15
1976	34,810	777	2.23	658	1.89	41	0.12	1,476	4.24
1977	36,722	844	2.30	658	1.79	36	0.10	1,538	4.19
1978	42,669	894	2.10	734	1.72	37	0.09	1,665	3.90
1979	48,373	1,076	2.22	808	1.67	59	0.12	1,943	4.02
1980	53,518	1,320	2.47	1,003	1.87	60	0.11	2,383	4.45
1981	56,993	1,445	2.54	1,193	2.09	90	0.16	2,728	4.79
1982	61,242	1,644	2.68	1,270	2.07	91	0.15	3,005	4.91
1983	65,971	1,862	2.82	1,534	2.33	97	0.15	3,493	5.29
1984	70,743	2,022	2.86	1,683	2.38	112	0.16	3,817	5.40
1985	71,564	2,043	2.85	1,731	2.42	109	0.15	3,883	5.43
1986	71,540	2,114	2.95	1,864	2.61	129	0.18	4,107	5.74
1987	69,171	2,182	3.15	1,840	2.66	149	0.22	4,171	6.03
1988	65,102	2,211	3.40	1,920	2.95	187	0.29	4,318	6.63
1989	62,572	2,122	3.39	1,996	3.19	192	0.31	4,310	6.89
1990	60,330	2,173	3.60	1,957	3.24	112	0.19	4,242	7.03
1991	63,466	2,304	3.63	2,125	3.35	146	0.23	4,575	7.21
1992	63,087	2,374	3.76	2,144	3.40	163	0.26	4,681	7.42
1993	64,455	2,637	4.09	2,310	3.58	175	0.27	5,122	7.95

*Source: National Action Council for Minorities in Engineering (NACME)

Appendix IX
Table of Fall Semester Freshmen Enrollments
in Engineering in California*

Academic Year	African American	Hispanic American	American Indian	Total Minority	Total Freshmen	Percent Minority
1973-74	81	74	0	155	3,607	4.30
1974-75	153	187	8	348	4,278	8.13
1975-76	169	234	8	411	5,332	7.71
1976-77	244	378	21	643	5,727	11.23
1977-78	297	419	26	742	6,083	12.20
1978-79	318	440	31	789	6,902	11.43
1979-80	316	511	34	861	7,311	11.78
1980-81	369	523	38	930	7,110	13.08
1981-82	354	613	61	1,028	8,085	12.71
1982-83	468	706	60	1,234	8,819	13.99
1983-84	386	714	38	1,138	8,420	13.52
1984-85	357	809	41	1,207	8,213	14.70
1985-86	289	690	53	1,032	8,002	12.90
1986-87	303	648	33	984	7,681	12.81
1987-88	303	778	37	1,118	8,031	13.92
1988-89	333	864	49	1,246	8,231	15.14
1989-90	345	879	62	1,286	8,195	15.69
1990-91	438	1,200	60	1,698	8,218	20.66
1991-92	355	1,143	67	1,565	7,780	20.12
1992-93	381	1,269	59	1,709	7,786	21.95

*Source: Engineering Workforce Commission of the American Association
of Engineering Societies (AAES)

Appendix X
Table of B.S. Degrees Granted to Minority Engineering Students in California Durring 1975-93*

Year	Total Degrees	African American No.	%	Hispanic American No.	%	American Indian No.	%	Total Minority No.	%
1975	2,755	45	1.63	137	4.97	5	0.18	187	6.79
1976	2,942	59	2.00	172	5.85	2	0.07	233	7.92
1977	3,205	57	1.78	156	4.87	2	0.06	215	6.71
1978	3,719	70	1.88	167	4.49	7	0.19	244	6.56
1979	4,279	61	1.43	165	3.86	5	0.12	231	5.40
1980	4,453	55	1.24	162	3.64	8	0.18	225	5.05
1981	4,946	56	1.19	197	3.98	6	0.12	259	5.24
1982	5,773	84	1.46	180	3.12	26	0.45	290	5.02
1983	5,482	124	2.26	288	5.25	12	0.22	424	7.73
1984	6,581	147	2.23	295	4.48	23	0.35	465	7.07
1985	6,437	138	2.14	334	5.19	16	0.25	488	7.58
1986	6,634	142	2.14	323	4.87	31	0.47	496	7.48
1987	7,041	165	2.34	404	5.74	32	0.45	601	8.54
1988	7,243	157	2.17	352	4.86	36	0.50	545	7.52
1989	7,263	167	2.30	445	6.13	35	0.48	648	8.92
1990	7,003	143	2.04	398	5.68	22	0.31	563	8.04
1991	6,697	154	2.30	507	7.57	30	0.45	691	10.32
1992	6,679	182	2.72	500	7.49	40	0.60	722	10.80
1993	6,967	169	2.41	527	7.56	33	0.47	729	10.46

*Source: Engineering Workforce Commission of the American Association of Engineering Societies (AAES)

Appendix XI
Table of MESA Statistics for the Years 1977-1993*

	1977-78	1978-79	1979-80	1980-81
HIGH SCHOOL				
No. of Centers	8	10	15	15
No. of Schools	23	44	77	93
No. of Students	819	1,442	2,092	2,104
No. of Graduates	113	272	413	664
Expenses	$144,490	$317,562	$545,823	$776,836
Cost per Student	$176	$220	$261	$369
UNIVERSITY				
No. of Colleges				
No. of Students				
No. of Graduates				
Expenses				
Cost per Student				
JUNIOR HIGH SCHOOL				
No. of Schools				
No. of Students				
Expenses				
Cost per Student				
ELEMENTARY SCHOOLS				
No. of Schools				
No. of Students				
Expenses				
Cost Per student				
STATEWIDE OFFICE STAFF				
No. of Staff	2	3	3	3
Expenses	$118,119	$163,888	$188,512	$253,314
Total No. of Students	819	1,442	2,092	2,104
Cost per Student	$144	$114	$90	$120
TOTAL EXPENSES	$262,609	$481,450	$734,335	$1,030,150
COST PER STUDENT	$321	$334	$351	$490

Table of MESA Statistics (Continued)

	1981-82	1982-83	1983-84	1984-85
HIGH SCHOOL				
No. of Centers	15	16	16	16
No. of Schools	102	115	140	142
No. of Students	2,519	3,096	3,820	3,962
No. of Graduates	785	890	1,204	1,122
Expenses	$821,009	$958,304	$1,036,250	$1,160,030
Cost per Student	$326	$310	$271	$293
UNIVERSITY				
No. of Colleges		14	15	15
No. of Students		1,115	2,143	2,393
No. of Graduates		0	201	195
Expenses		$285,000	$532,000	$626,254
Cost per Student		$256	$254	$262
JUNIOR HIGH SCHOOL				
No. of Schools				19
No. of Students				550
Expenses				$77,504
Cost per Student				$141
ELEMENTARY SCHOOLS				
No. of Schools				
No. of Students				
Expenses				
Cost Per student				
STATEWIDE OFFICE STAFF				
No. of Staff	6	8	11	12
Expenses	$292,136	$532,617	$598,701	$658,073
Total No. of Students	2,519	4,211	5,963	6,905
Cost per Student	$116	$126	$100	$95
TOTAL EXPENSES	$1,113,145	$1,850,921	$2,261,007	$2,608,331
COST PER STUDENT	$442	$440	$379	$378

Table of MESA Statistics (Continued)

	1985-86	1986-87	1987-88	1988-89
HIGH SCHOOL				
No. of Centers	16	17	17	17
No. of Schools	134	127	135	123
No. of Students	4,176	3,108	3,409	3,964
No. of Graduates	815	778	850	604
Expenses	$1,252,150	$957,180	$1,014,272	$993,060
Cost per Student	$300	$308	$298	$250
UNIVERSITY				
No. of Colleges	15	16	17	18
No. of Students	2,644	2,488	3,006	3,173
No. of Graduates	117	209	351	460
Expenses	$638,101	$635,181	$763,000	$800,751
Cost per student	$241	$255	$254	$252
JUNIOR HIGH SCHOOL				
No. of Schools	28	40	45	69
No. of Students	1,008	1,036	1,366	1,914
Expenses	$125,920	$243,082	$366,841	$346,658
Cost per Student	$125	$234	$268	$181
ELEMENTARY SCHOOLS				
No. of Schools				11
No. of Students				128
STATEWIDE OFFICE STAFF				
No. of Staff	12	10	11	15
Expenses	$741,808	$680,705	$736,173	$973,542
Total no. of Students	7,828	6,632	7,781	9,179
Cost per Student	$95	$102	$95	$106
TOTAL EXPENSES	$2,757,979	$2,516,148	$2,880,286	$3,114,011
COST PER STUDENT	$352	$379	$370	$339

Table of MESA Statistics (Continued)

	1989-90	1990-91	1991-92	1992-93
HIGH SCHOOL				
No. of Centers	20	20	20	20
No. of Schools	121	125	133	135
No. of Students	4,843	5,764	6,277	6,851
No. of Graduates	680	1,022	1,183	1,347
Expenses	$982,738	$796,165	$804,223	$798,452
Cost per Student	$203	$138	$128	$117
UNIVERSITY				
No. of Colleges	18	26	23	23
No. of Students	3,524	3,942	4,983	4,945
No. of Graduates	505	537	665	587
Expenses	$771,969	$728,349	$725,135	$731,376
Cost per student	$219	$185	$160	$148
JUNIOR HIGH SCHOOL				
No. of Schools	81	95	92	95
No. of Students	2,658	3,273	3,506	3,944
Expenses	$399,152	$528,551	$371,336	$488,390
Cost per Student	$150	$161	$106	$124
ELEMENTARY SCHOOLS				
No. of Schools	15	30	28	36
No. of Students	281	841	696	1,288
STATEWIDE OFFICE STAFF				
No. of Staff	14	13	15	14
Expenses	$1,090,460	$1,260,714	$985,707	$1,295,750
Total no. of Students	11,306	13,820	15,462	17,028
Cost per Student	$96	$91	$64	$76
TOTAL EXPENSES	$3,241,319	$3,417,787	$3,067,719	$3,460,951
COST PER STUDENT	$287	$247	$198	$203

*Source: MESA California

Apendix XII
List of Programs Nationwide Based on MESA Model*

AZ-MESA Project
P.O. Box 40400
Tucson, AZ 85717

CMEA (Colorado Minority Engineeing
  Association)
College of Engineering
University of Colorado at Denver
P.O. Box 104
Denver, CO 80217-3364
303/556-2344

Connecticut Pre-Engineering Program
950 Trout Brook Drive
W. Hartford, CN 06119
203/231-2824, Ext. 20

DAPCEP (Detroit Area Pre-College
  Engineering Program)
Rackman Educational Memorial Building
60 Farnsworth
Detroit, MI 48202
313/831-3050

MACESA (Mid-America Consortium for
  Engineering and Science Achievement)
Kansas State University
144 Durland Hall
Manhattan, KS 66506
800/882-0018

MassPEP (Massachusetts Pre-Engineering
  Program, Inc.)
Wentworth Institute of Technology
553 Huntington Avenue
Boston, MA 02155
617/427-7227

MSEN (Mathematics and Science
  Education Network)
University of North Carolina
201 Peabody Hall
Chapel Hill, NC 27599
919/966-3256

MD-MESA
The Johns Hopkins University
Applied Physics Laboratory
Johns Hopkins Road
Laurel, MD 20723
301/953-5380

NM-MESA
Ferris Center 137
Albuquerque, NM 87131
505/277-5831

NV-Minority Engineering Program
University of Nevada at Las Vega
Las Vegas, NV

NY-MESA
NYC-Stony Brook
Stony Brook, NY

OR-MESA
Portland State University
P.O. Box 751
Portland, OR 97207
503/299-4665

SD-MESA
South Dakota School of Mines & Technology
501 E Street
Rapid City, SD 57701-3995

UT-MESA
Educational Equity
Utah State Office of Education
250 East 500 South
Salt Lake City, UT 84111
801/538-7648

WA-MESA
College of Engineering
University of Washington
353 Loew FH-18
Seattle, WA 98195
206/543-0562

*Source: MESA-California

Index

Subject Index